Wombourne Worthies

British Library Cataloguing in Publication Data
A catalogue record is available for this book from the British Library

ISBN 978-0-9930073-4-7

Every effort has been made to seek permission to reproduce the images contained in this book, and we are grateful to the many individuals and institutions who have assisted in this task. Any omissions are entirely unintentional, and if addressed to the publishers will gladly be amended in future editions.

Ellingham Press, 43 High Street, Much Wenlock, Shropshire TF13 6AD
www.ellinghampress.co.uk

Cover by Aardvark Illustration & Design
www.aardvarkid.com

Typesetting by ISB Typesetting, Sheffield
www.sheffieldtypesetting.co.uk

Wombourne Worthies:

And those who were not

Wombourne History Group

Ellingham Press

Dedication

To all local historians, past, present and future

To the memory of W.G. Hoskins who first inspired us all to look at our local history, its landscape, and the towns and villages which sit in that landscape and who made research into local history 'respectable'.

To his worthy successors, notably Professor Michael Wood, whose enthusiasm and ability to communicate his own passion for the subject encourages and sustains us all, amateurs and professionals alike, to continue to explore and record our own locality.

To those who will follow us, in the hope that they get as much fun out of their research as we do!

Contents

Picture Credits

P 5 Will of John Spittle courtesy of Staffordshire & Stoke on Trent Archive Service, Lichfield Record Office.

Pp 11 and 12 The arms of Emmanuel College Cambridge, and Emmanuel College in 1690, by kind permission of the archivist, Emmanuel College Cambridge to reproduce the images relating to the college in general and specifically Ithiel Smart.

Pp 14 and 16 Ithiel Smart entries in the Wombourne Parish Registers courtesy of Staffordshire Record Office.

Pp 21 and 22 Daniell Smart's christening entry by permission of the LMA, the custodians of the register.

P 28 Silver dish courtesy of Margaret King.

P 31 Entry in the marriage register for Richard Tomlinson and Mary Jones, 7 July 1834 by kind permission of Staffordshire Record Office.

Pp 34 and 35 The 1710 Apprenticeship Indenture for Richard Powell by kind permission of The National Archives.

P 42 Policemen in the 1860s by kind permission of Newcastle under Lyme Borough Council.

P 43 Sword used in 1842 by kind permission of Newcastle under Lyme Borough Council.

P 48 Policeman's truncheon reproduced courtesy of Stephen L. Hofgartner at Hungerford Antiques.

P 50 Burslem Police Force by kind permission of Newcastle under Lyme Borough Council.

P 56 Hand-drawn map courtesy of David Taylor.

P 66 Map from an auctioneer's catalogue 1910.

P 70 Goodyear's steel wheels by kind permission of Dudley Archives and Local History Service.

Picture Credits

P 73 Juvenile beekeepers reproduced from *Around Pattingham & Wombourne* by May Griffiths, Peter Leigh and Mary Mills published by Allan Sutton Publishers, 1992.

P 75 John Apse in his 80s by kind permission of May Griffiths.

P 78 School staff prior to First World War by kind permission of May Griffiths.

P 79 Mrs Apse and her cookery class reproduced from *Wombourne What Was* by May Griffiths, Uralia Press, 1990.

P 80 First XI Cricket Team and 1st XI Football Team by kind permission of May Griffiths.

P 83 John Apse in one of Wombourne's first cars reproduced from *Around Pattingham & Wombourne* by May Griffiths, Peter Leigh and Mary Mills published by Allan Sutton Publishers, 1992.

Acknowledgements

My personal thanks go to the following:

Samantha Beeston, Archivist at the Wallace Collection, London, for her help over the Wombourne silver dish; also to the curators of the Wallace Collection for information about the origins of the dish and for permission to reproduce their caption attached to the exhibit when on show in their collection.

Andrew George, Principal Archivist at Lichfield, for not only answering many of my queries but teaching me different ways of finding answers for myself.

Amanda Goode, Archivist of Emmanuel College Cambridge, for her patient help in providing information and material about Ithiel Smart.

May Griffiths, MBE for help with the text about John Apse and permission to use photographs of him and his family.

Dr Nigel Tringham, Senior Lecturer at Keele University and County Editor of Victoria County History of Staffordshire, for encouragement and a valuable critique of the article on Ithiel Smart.

Above all, my thanks are due to my colleagues and friends in WHiG, who tolerate my editorial bullying and who, when asked to produce papers at very short notice, did so with apparent ease and great good humour.

They are the real heroes of this book and are indeed true *WOMBOURNE WORTHIES*.

The Editor

Foreword

For an archivist, one of the great pleasures of picking up a work of local history is knowing that the records we carefully collect and preserve have been used, sometimes exhaustively used, in its production. That pleasure is further rather selfishly enhanced when decent references have been given to sources, to enable future researchers to check, corroborate and occasionally develop the lines of enquiry laid out.

The authors themselves may be well known to us as regular users and note-takers in our search rooms and libraries. Increasingly, they will have identified just what they want from our online catalogues, ordered in advance, and come armed with a digital camera to get the most out of a single visit, once they have managed to find a parking space or negotiated the vagaries of public transport. They can often be the people who enhance our public service by their willingness to share.

What we rarely know at that point is what if anything will happen to the results of their labour. We hope that, as here, it will be made available in some form for others, to inform and preferably to entertain too. Increasingly, we in the Archive Service will be looking to them as our partners to get our message out there into the communities of Staffordshire.

The reason lying behind all this is the knowledge that the stories of individuals, high and low, can illuminate the history of a place. In this case, they make it come alive over a period of four centuries. Clergymen and teachers, policemen and pub landlords all potentially have stories to tell. The written records may not tell us all we want to know. School logbooks can be a tremendous source, but they reflect the interests and concerns of the specific head teacher. Individual pupils, in many cases, are only likely to get a mention if they have been particularly good (perhaps gaining a scholarship) or bad (found fighting in the playground).

I don't believe I'm related to Alf George, a competitor comedian to Sam Redfern (page 63), but I'm now tempted to try to find out something about him – and that sort of chance discovery is one of the delights of a book like this.

Andrew George

Introduction

Selecting people for this book was not easy. Dust has to settle before any sort of assessment can be made as to who might be 'worthy' (or not), so the decision was made to exclude most people who had been personally known to us.

One prime candidate for inclusion was Sir Samuel Hellier of the Wombourne Wodehouse who, in true eighteenth-century fashion, aspired to great things. Amongst other achievements he redesigned the gardens at the Wombourne Wodehouse and, having a passion for music, built and equipped the Music Room there. One of his more eccentric ideas was to emulate some of his grander neighbours in the Midland shires by having an orchestra made up of local people. However, I had already done some research for Martin Perkins at the Birmingham Conservatoire in connection with his PhD on Sir Samuel, so I reluctantly abandoned him to greater academic needs. There were many other more conventional worthies who probably qualified but were rejected in the interests of being 'just too worthy', if not downright dull.

There is a woeful shortage of women. Lively courtesans or even a wicked stepmother do not appear in Wombourne's records, although there are many ladies who did much good work in the parish. A touch of spice was required.

Outright villains were also hard to apprehend; even David Taylor's Policemen failed to bag more than a couple of fowl thieves. Famous highwaymen? Not in Wombourne. Mill-burning in 1814 sounded promising, but although it was thought to be arson no one was ever held to account for it. Even the maid at Heath Mill who bought a stolen bible from John Duncalf in 1677 for three shillings (a vast sum of money for a maid to have at that time – how did she have so much?) may not have known she was a receiver of stolen goods. Swindon, which was for a time in Wombourne parish, produced likely candidates. One was William Hawkswood, convicted and hanged in 1807 for poisoning his master, as well as the men who burned barley ricks in 1831. Alas, I found them too late to do the necessary research. The

Gunpowder Plotters belong to yet another village, just south of the Wombourne parish border. Holbeache House, where the last few conspirators made their last stand, lies in Himley, and stealing Himley's glory would not have been neighbourly. Jenny Davies's gang of 1563 brawled at Bobbington, which is well outside the parish boundaries, but they came so fully prepared with protests of their innocence that they were irresistible. The detailed account of their case makes splendid reading and justifies the compound title of the book.

Ultimately, local historians are today's hunter-gatherers: they follow the trail of their prey through the archives and old newspapers, make the kill (*'Eureka! I found it!'*) and share the spoil with their tribe. We hope you enjoy the resultant feast.

A Brawl at Bobbington in 1534

Jennifer Davies

In early 1535, Ralph Broke, a gentleman from Bobbington, complained to the Court of Star Chamber of Henry VIII that on 8 December 1534, when he, his brother Michael Broke, and an assistant, Thomas Bailey, were quietly minding cattle on the New Rudding at Bobbington, land owned by Ralph Broke's father, John Broke of Blakelands, they were violently assaulted and detained by a group of ruffians. He demanded that those responsible be committed to the Fleet prison for riotous behaviour.

The organiser of the assault was Humphrey Spittle, the bailiff of a local landowner, Sir Giles Strangways. Humphrey had incited various members of his family, including four of his sons (Hugh, a farmer at the nearby Meyr, and Richard, Thomas and William), as well as his son-in-law John Watkis, to join with Humphrey and John Taylor, William Tyrry and Thomas Kirkham to form a vigilante squad armed with staves and bows and arrows. William Spittle's presence in this gang may have been partially due to him being employed as the chantry priest of the Blessed Mary at Enville church, to sing a service every day at the altar of Our Lady for the souls of benefactors, and that post had been granted to him by Sir Giles Strangways.[1] Despite William Spittle and his brother Hugh being the two menacingly armed with bows and arrows, a local farmer, Richard Clare of the Meyr, in his will of 20 July 1537, still bequeathed him eight marks, 'to pray for me and my family for one year following my departing'.[2]

Broke maintained that he and his companions had been so terrified of the armed Spittle band that they had (rather surprisingly) allowed them to come too close to them. He had been beaten to the ground, with his head split open, before Thomas Bailey, fearing that Ralph and Michael were about to be killed, had, with great difficulty, managed to escape to the nearby community of the Meyr to raise the alarm. In fact, against their wills, the brothers had been taken a mile to Humphrey Spittle's dwelling at Enville. A posse of John Dasshesen, aged 58 years, Thomas Dasshesen, curate at Enville church, aged 47 years,

Lewis Clare, aged 50 years, and Nicholas Moseley, aged 43 years, then came to the rescue. However, Humphrey Spittle asserted that he was within his rights, and insisted upon keeping the Broke brothers in custody. Subsequently, a witness reported that William Tyrry of Spittle's assault party was indignant at being indicted for riot, as the group had only been acting under the command of Humphrey Spittle. Furthermore, whilst he had been holding Ralph by one arm and Humphrey Taylor had been holding him by the other, Richard Spittle would have slain him if he had not pulled Ralph backwards.

The Spittles in defence swore their answer before Sir John Gifford, knight, and Walter Wrottesley, esquire, that April. They maintained they were not guilty of any riot, and that this action had been brought to put them to unjust costs, and to draw a veil over the multitude of offences of not only Ralph and Michael Broke and Thomas Bailey, but also of their purported rescuers. The case might result in unfair loss to Sir Giles Strangways, landowner of the manor of Lutley at Enville, and even place his ownership of his land in jeopardy.

They stated that Sir Giles Strangways had inherited 200 acres of ground with buildings and an orchard in the manor of Lutley, at Clare Heys. This had been let 'time out of mind' by Sir Giles and his ancestors to farmers and other lessees who had quietly enjoyed the property. That was until about two years before, when Thomas Dasshesen, priest, and other adherents of the Brokes, had wilfully 'cast down' large parts of the hedges and had wrecked the ditches. They had even, under the direction of Ralph Broke, set fire to a hedge and damaged the wall of the house. Under the circumstances, Sir Giles had behaved most reasonably towards the culprits, and being assured by their promise of future good behaviour, had taken only modest amends, and he himself had paid for a new hedge to be set. However, he had also instructed his bailiff, Humphrey Spittle, to keep a nightly watch so anyone attempting to destroy any hedges in future might be apprehended and sued. Humphrey Spittle had received intelligence that an offensive on the property was planned for the night of 8 December 1534, so accordingly he had organised his party to lie in wait peacefully to protect the new hedge and to catch those intending mischief. At about ten o'clock that night they caught sight of Ralph and Michael Broke and Thomas Bailey, with their supporters, about two miles from their own homes, in the act of spoiling the hedge. Without using any violence, the group detained Ralph and Michael, and took them to the house of Humphrey Spittle, to question them. Here they spent a pleasant two hours sitting by the fire, eating and drinking, before leaving quietly. Furthermore, any hurt which Ralph Broke had received inadvertently had been caused by himself. However, it was rather odd for the Brokes to have been entertained so agreeably by Humphrey Spittle.

Walter Wrottesley and another local gentleman, John Gravenour, acting on the king's authority, heard and examined witnesses about this matter at Trysull on June 24, 1535. Firstly, William Billingsley of Ludstone, aged 49 years, claimed that a few days before the affray, Ralph Broke and Hugh Spittle had quarrelled in Wolverhampton. Secondly, Humphrey Wolverley of Bobbington, aged 50 years, stated that he had witnessed Hugh Spittle serving Ralph Broke with a subpoena in Bobbington church and that Ralph had accused Hugh of, in a sly manner, 'taking him like a thief'.

The Star Chamber under Henry VIII frequently dealt with cases of assault, and also ones involving the enclosure of open land, which was causing contention in Staffordshire at that time. However expressed, the basis of many disputes was property ownership. This was borne out in this case by most of the witness statements, taken from mature men of some standing in the community. Apart from those named in this report there were another thirty-four who corroborated the assertions of earlier witnesses. Most lived in the immediate vicinity of the enclosed land, with nine witnesses from over the border in Shropshire, two from Himley, three from Seisdon, two from Swindon, and one from Trysull. In his original complaint, Ralph Broke stated that Clare Heys, where the fracas took place, 'ought to lie in common' for the use of the communities of Lutley and the Meyr, but had lately been enclosed by Hugh Spittle and others, contrary to right. Indeed, there was general consensus among the witnesses that this common land had been enclosed in living memory. William Billingsley stated that for forty years past he knew Clare Heyes to lie in common until William Bullwardyn had enclosed it about three years before. Thomas Whorwood of the Morfe, gentleman, aged 88 years, knew Clare Heyes to lie open for eighty years past, until some years since when William Bullwardyn enclosed it. In agreement, John Crosway of the Morfe, aged 70 years, said his father was 100 years old and had died thirty years before. All their lives they had dwelt half a mile from Clare Heyes; his father had never known it enclosed. Richard Dasshesen of Enville, aged 73 years, said he had known the ground for sixty years and in that time it was never enclosed, nor was there a house with an orchard there, until William Bullwardyn enclosed it. Finally, Richard Howlatt of Bobbington, aged 72 years, stated that for 'about sixty years past he [had] dwelt with a gentlewoman called Mistress Sowden, and being her servant, he oft times fetched her horse in the said common'. The other issue witnesses reported on was whether Ralph Broke's party had destroyed any hedges on the night of 8 December 1534, which they had denied. It appears that only two witnesses categorically stated that the hedges were as whole as they had been the previous morning, Lewis Clare, who was in the alleged rescue party, and Thomas Lea of the Hoo, gentleman, aged 28 years, who said that he had seen no hedges broken or moved. Finally, rather dubiously, two men from Enville both admitted to paying Thomas Dasshesen the curate some money in connection with the incident, but did not say why.

The outcome of this case at the Court of Star Chamber is unrecorded. Possibly worn down by this action, Sir Giles Strangways, knight, sold his holdings in the area, before he died aged 58 in 1546.[3] The main beneficiary was the justice and ex-High Sheriff who had heard the case in Staffordshire, Walter Wrottesley. In November 1540 he paid £340 for land at Lutley, Meyr, Morfe and Enville, and he also obtained the lands and priest's house belonging to the chantry of the Blessed Mary at Enville church.[4] Despite William Spittle's involvement in the affray investigated by Walter Wrottesley, he remained as chantry priest, taking most of the chantry rental income as his salary until 1548 when Edward VI's government pensioned off the chantry priests, whilst dismantling those bulwarks of Catholicism, the chantries. Another who gained was Ralph Broke: in November 1540 he paid £60 for land at Bobbington.

Humphrey Spittle had died by September 1540, as it was in that month that his will was proved.[5] In a lengthy document in which he stated that he wished to be buried 'before my seat whereas I do kneel within the high church of Enville', he apportioned his property between his son John, who was his heir, his other sons Richard, Hugh and Thomas, and his son-in-law John Watkis. He stipulated that his son William, a priest, should have 'his table and board freely with his heir John', and that if the opportunity arose he should have 'a gown and a bed seemly for a priest to lie in'. John was not happy with his father's will. In his will written in 1553 witnessed by several men including Richard Whorewood, the parson of Enville, he bequeathed money to maintain the church, and 20s. to be given out on the day of his burial, probably with the expectation of obtaining prayers for his soul. He also gave 20s. to each of his brothers Richard and Thomas, and gifts to several neighbours, including one of a quantity of rye to William Tyrry, the member of the party who had been aggrieved at being indicted for assault. John's final statement after the witnesses to his will had been named was 'as touching my father's will I am content and agreeable to the same'.[6]

Thomas Dasshesen continued as curate writing Enville wills into the late 1540s; in 1537, as 'his ghostly father', he was bequeathed 20s. by Richard Clare to oversee the execution of his will. Thomas Kirkham, who was also implicated in the affray, had become churchwarden of Enville church by 1553, and advised Edward VI's commissioners about which ornaments and ceremonial artefacts the church possessed.

The conclusion of John Spittle's will which says *and these ar wyttnes of my last wyll John Hackett clarke John Lyttley John Tayler Master Richard Whorewod p[ar]son of Enfold and as tochinge my fathers will I am content and agreable to the same.*

Although women were fortunate in that none were involved in the affray and hence subsequent legal action, their position was subordinate to that of men. No woman was cited as a witness, let alone acted as a magistrate! Was it really the case that no woman saw or heard anything of relevance to this incident? Wills were written to ensure that heirs received the bulk of the family estate, not to protect the livelihood of widows. In his will written in 1550, a relative of Ralph Broke, Humphrey Broke, a farmer of modest means, left £10 to his three children, who were to receive the money when they were seventeen years old. He added that if 'my wife Pernelle do marry before the children be paid then ... she [to] put in sufficient surety for the payment of £10 before she marry or else ... Ralph Broke and Richard Pryste do take of the goods into their hands of the value of £10 for the payment of my children'. This was all very well, but the total value of the goods listed on his inventory, 'the day of his death', was £11 4s. This included livestock: horses, cows, swine, hens and geese, and his household goods.

It can be seen from the map inside the front cover that the affray occurred in a relatively remote area of Staffordshire, near the border with Shropshire. Contemporary inventories reveal that transport, if not on foot, was by horse, or a wagon drawn by oxen, which most farmers possessed. About three years later the Reformation began in earnest when Thomas Cromwell effected the Dissolution of the Monasteries, including the closure and destruction of Dudley Priory about eight miles away. Virtually everyone in Staffordshire, considered to have been a rural backwater which adhered to traditional ways,[7] was still Catholic, as revealed by Enville wills, which all began with the testator committing their soul to Almighty God, Our Lady Saint Mary, and All the Holy Company of Heaven. People believed that life was a journey towards death, and that after death most were condemned to a period in purgatory, where sinners were cleansed through suffering, assisted by the prayers of the living and intercession of saints. Priests, through whom one could approach God and shorten one's time in purgatory, held positions of great authority within local communities. Humphrey Spittle referred to acquiring a bed for his son William 'seemly for a priest to lie in'. Despite the church being the focus of village life and the importance attached to the religious aspect of one's existence, this incident reveals that actions such as violence towards individuals, and appropriation and destruction of property, did not give rise to general opprobrium; and that women were universally undervalued. For instance, Richard Clare of the Meyr had no compunction in 1537 about bequeathing both William Spittle eight marks to pray for him and his family, and Thomas Dasshesen 20s. to oversee his will. Overall, the incident certainly aroused considerable interest in the surrounding area, as about forty witnesses gave evidence, travelling to Trysull from as far afield as Stourbridge, and yet the perpetrators appear to have sailed through it with impunity.

References

Information extracted from:

W. Boyd, 'Staffordshire suits in the Court of Star Chamber temp. Henry VII and Henry VIII abstracted from the original documents in the Public Records Office', *Collections for a History of Staffordshire*, The William Salt Archaeological Society, New Series, Vol. X, part 1 (1907), pp. 141–43.

W. Boyd, 'Star Chamber proceedings. Henry VIII and Edward VI', *Collections for a History of Staffordshire*, The William Salt Archaeological Society, Third Series (1912), pp. 71–75.

Sixteenth-century spelling and punctuation have been changed to present-day conventions.

Notes

1 W. N. Landor, 'Staffordshire incumbents and parochial records (1530–1680)', *Collections for a History of Staffordshire*, The William Salt Archaeological Society, Third Series (1915), pp. 98–101.

2 Will of Richard Clare of Enville (Lichfield Record Office, proved *c.*1537). A mark was worth 13s. 4d.

3 H. Miller, 'Strangways, Sir Giles (1486–1546), of Melbury Sampford, Dorset', in *History of Parliament Online*, The Institute of Historical Research, Members, 1508–1558.

4 G. Wrottesley, 'The final concords or feet of fines, Staffordshire, 21–38, Henry VIII, 176, 178', in *Collections for a History of Staffordshire*, The William Salt Archaeological Society, Third Series (1911), pp. 269–92.

5 Will of Humphrey Spittle of Enville (Lichfield Record Office, proved 27 September 1540).

6 Will of John Spittle of Enville (Lichfield Record Office, proved 24 January 1554).

7 D. M. Palliser, 'Popular reactions to the Reformation during the years of uncertainty 1530–70', in C. Haigh (ed.), *The English Reformation Revised* (Cambridge University Press, Cambridge, 1987), p. 105.

Ithiel Smart: Vicar of Wombourne

'A Famous Divine and a painful preacher'

c.1598–22 November 1661

Margaret King

Ithiel's story starts in the small Northamptonshire village of Preston Capes, where his father, Robert SMARTE, was vicar in the latter part of the reign of Queen Elizabeth I.

Robert SMART (without the E) was baptised on 24 June 1546 in Clifford Chambers, Warwickshire, ordained deacon in Peterborough on 3 July 1573 and, assuming that there are not two clerics of the same name at the same time, he was 'installed as Perpetual Vicar* of Preston Capes, Northamptonshire on 30 June 1585'.[1] His patron was Sir Robert LANE† who was a known Protestant, so there can be little doubt that Robert SMARTE followed the same way of thinking. He is said to have been married to Katherine (surname unknown), but no marriage details are known. We also do not know how many children they actually had, but they founded a dynasty of dissenting clerics, amongst whom are Nathaniel, born in 1590, Ezekial (or other variations of the spelling), date of birth unknown, Elisha, born and died in 1593, and Ithiel, born about 1598.‡ The three surviving sons

* **Perpetual** This term originated from 'perpetual curacy'. Once licensed, clergy could not be removed by their nominating patron and could only be deprived by their diocesan bishop through ecclesiastical courts.

† **Sir Robert LANE 1527–*c*.1588** of Horton, Northants. A substantial figure in Northamptonshire, and classified in 1564 as an 'earnest furtherer' of religion, with access to Bishop Parker: i.e. he was one of those intent on reforming the Church. He was a Justice of the Peace, an ecclesiastical Commissioner for the dioceses of Lincoln and Peterborough in 1571, but selling much property by 1580. *Source: History of Parliament.*

‡ **Names of SMART sons** Nathaniel; Ezekial; Elisha: a prophet; Ithiel: (probably) 'God is with me'.

in their turn gave their own sons the same Old Testament names of prophets or famous Israelite leaders, which leads to much confusion. The years of their birth remain unconfirmed and are to be treated with some caution. The parish registers in Preston Capes are missing until 1614, so there are no records to confirm the baptism of these children.*

After installation, Robert SMART's name appears only in wills, twice as the recipient of small sums of money (in two wills,[2] dated 1599 and 1601, of people living in Preston Capes), but also as overseer of the will of Thomas BUCKBY on 23 April 1602 for which he was to receive 'a ewe or 6s. 8d'. This is an odd phrase because there was by that time a parish post of 'overseer': an overseer of the poor is not the same as the overseer of a will.

Times were particularly hard during the first few years of the seventeenth century. Plague had returned again, bringing death in its wake, and the weather was exceptionally cold (in London the Thames froze over) with heavy snow, ice and rainfall. The winter of 1606–07 was the worst of all. In the countryside, harvests were poor for years in succession following cold winters and heavy rain and in Northamptonshire violence and rioting flared up sporadically, mainly against the enclosure of common land for sheep farming, but also against the many other changes forced upon the people. Not least of these was the Poor Relief Act of 1601 which tried to deal with the problems arising from collapse of charities after the Dissolution of the Monasteries. Hence the need for an 'overseer'.

However, 'Perpetual Vicar' Robert was not to be: '... on 4 July 1605 George Webb BA installed on depriv. of John SMART'.[3] (There is no clerical John SMART in any of the records so perhaps this is a transcription error.) Why he was 'deprived' is not stated although a search in the bishop's visitations might give a clue. He may have defied the bishop by refusing to comply with one of the many requirements of the 1604 Canons or upset someone in authority; perhaps his Puritan face did not fit, but whatever the cause he was put out of his living. Searches in the Northamptonshire County Archives reveal no further mention of him, nor any members of his family. Wherever they went it must have been very hard for the family and have left a lasting impression on Ithiel and his siblings. Despite the upheaval, someone ensured that the SMART boys, wherever they spent their youth, received a good classically-based education. This might have

* **BMD Registers** In 1538 Thomas Cromwell, Henry VIII's Chancellor, ordered that all parishes should keep Registers of Baptisms, Marriages and Burials, so these should be known, more properly, as BMB Registers. Since 1837 Registers of Births, Marriages and Deaths have been kept centrally and are usually known as BMD.

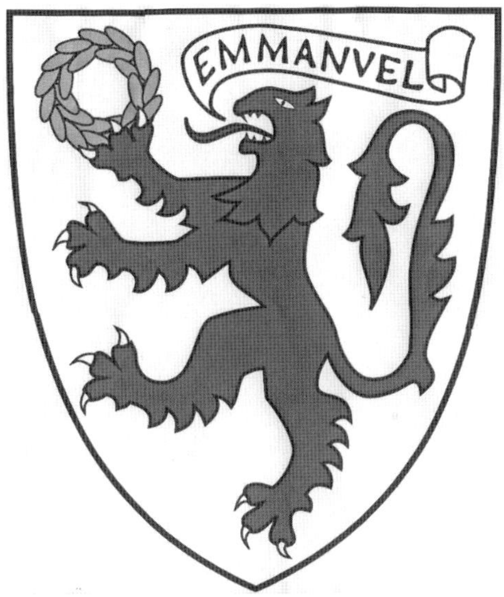

The arms of Emmanuel College, Cambridge.

been at home but this was also the heyday of good, local grammar schools which existed in many small market towns. They educated clever boys, even from humble backgrounds, to a very high standard and the boys might well have attended one of these before going on to university.

The first authenticated record of Ithiel Smart is his signature in the Admission Register of Emmanuel College Cambridge where he was admitted sizar on 3 March 1617 (*not* on the 8th as is generally given). A sizar was a poor scholar admitted to a college in return for 'domestic duties'. As his admission to Emmanuel College in 1617 is not in doubt his birth date just might be. Nineteen would have been quite 'old' at a time when young men often matriculated aged 15–16, so it is possible that he was born in 1601/2 rather than three years earlier.

Emmanuel College was founded in 1584 by a Puritan, Sir Walter Mildmay, Chancellor of the Exchequer to Elizabeth I, 'for the education of puritan ministers'. It occupied the site of a Dominican friary which had been partially demolished following the Dissolution of the Monasteries. By 1617 the old Dominican chapel was being used as the dining hall and the friars' dining hall as a Puritan chapel. Little now remains of the buildings that Ithiel would have used; much of the college was rebuilt first by Sir Christopher Wren, again in 1690 and at intervals thereafter.

Ithiel Smart matriculated in 1617, became BA 1620–21 and MA in 1624. He was ordained deacon in 1622 in Lichfield.[4] But if he was fully ordained in 1625, where was he between that date and 1632?

Emmanuel College in 1690.

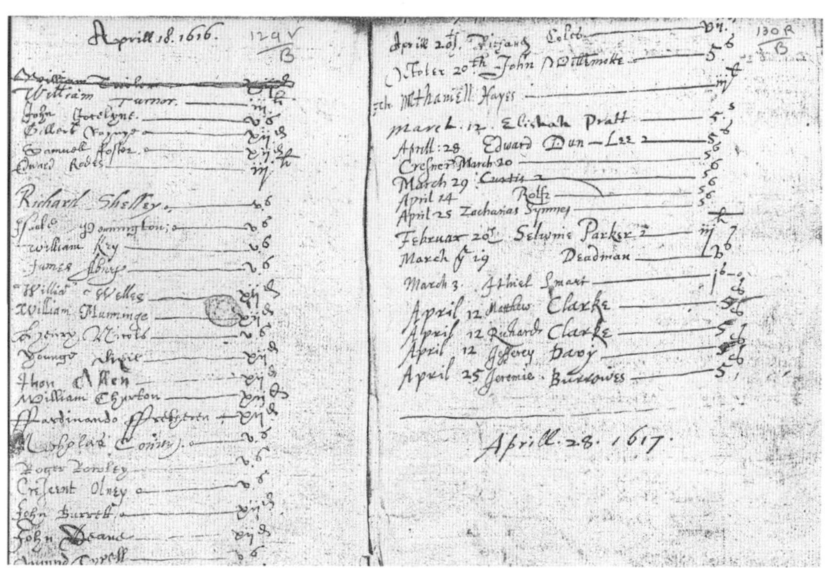

The register of Emmanuel College showing Ithiel Smart's signature March 3rd 1616.

For in that year he reappears, appointed vicar of Womborne[5] in succession to Anthony HAMNETT, buried on 19 August 1632, who 'had been vicar 38 years'. It seems increasingly likely that he spent those years in London, but no trace of him has been found to support this theory, except for the connection of the lay Patron who presented him for the living at Wombourne. This was John Wollaston, gent., later Sir John. He was a freeman and goldsmith of the City of London, who became Lord Mayor of London in 1638. The Wollaston family, originally from Tettenhall, lived at Trescott some four miles north-west of Wombourne. They held the right of presentation to the living at Wombourne having bought it from Edward, Lord Dudley. There is no obvious connection between the two men from birth or upbringing (different counties); Wollaston did not go to Cambridge, so the city of London seems more than likely.

Wherever he had been the new incumbent must have looked over his 'new patch' with a more than somewhat jaundiced eye. He wrote what he thought about the previous management on the very first page of a Register of Baptisms, Marriages and Deaths.[6]

This leather-bound book opens with a diplomatic statement acknowledging Ithiel Smart's debt to Sir John. Courtesies observed, he gets down to business.

He comments scathingly on the first page about the poor record-keeping of his predecessor and he recopies some older records dated 1570, presumably from records now lost. Comparing his writing in Wombourne's records with that of his signature in the admission register of Emmanuel College there can be little doubt that the hand is the same. The college had until now been uncertain as to whether the entry in their register might have made by a clerk. We are doubly fortunate in that he wrote in a hand which is easily read. Another entry in the book, which reads more like churchwardens' accounts, starts with an elegantly designed and laid-out entry in sonorous Latin: '*Ithiel Smart in artibus magister colleg. Eman Cantabrigiensis quondam alumnis inductus fuit in corporalem ... posessionem vicars de Womborne & Tresle Aug alt 1632 ... anno atatis ...*' This well-educated Cambridge scholar was not averse to displaying his good command of a classical language.

Scholar he undoubtedly was, but not of the vague and unobservant kind, and he was in no mind to suffer fools, gladly or otherwise. His first act was to sack the parish clerk: 'James Hughes put out of the Clarke's place...and William Cartwright put in'. The clerk's was an important post in parish life, acting almost as deputy to the vicar. The canons of 1604 required him 'to be of honest conversation and sufficient for his reading, writing and also for his competent skill in singing, if it may be'. In which of these Ithiel found James Hughes wanting is not recorded. Perhaps William Cartwright had a better voice.

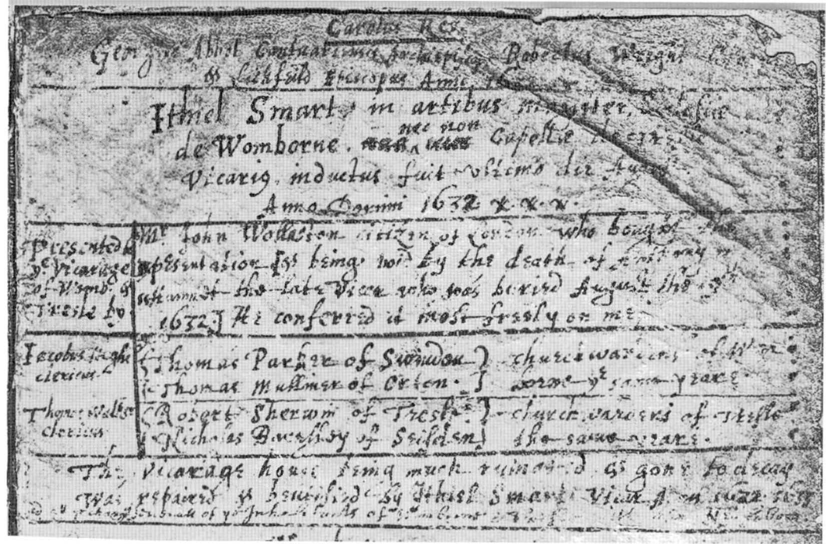

Carolus R...

Georgius Abbot Cantuariensis Archiepiscopus ... Robertus Wright ...
& Lichfeld Episcopus Ann...

Ithiel Smart in artibus magister, Ecclesie de Wombórne nec non Capellie de Tresle Vicarius inductus fuit ultimo die Au... Anno Domini 1632 ...

Presented ye Vicarage of Womborne & Tresle by	Mr John Wollaston citizen of London who bought the presentation (it being void by the death of [illegible] the late Vicar who was buried August the 13th 1632) he conferred it most freely on me.
Jacobus Hughes clericus	Thomas Parker of Swindon } Thomas Mullener of Orton } churchwardens of Womborne ye same yeare
[illegible] clericus	Robert Sherwin of Tresle } Nicholas Barnsley of Seisdon } churchwardens of Tresle the same yeare.

The Vicarage house being much ruinated & gone to decay was repaired & beautified by Ithiel Smart Vicar Anno 1632 1633 [illegible]

Ithiel Smart's first entry in the register of St Benedict Biscop, Wombourne 1632.

James Hughes put out of the Clarkes place, & William Cartwright Nayler was put in the same Ano Domini 1632.
Mr Abraham Barwicke = [1633] = Curate of Womborne and Tresle two yeares
Anno Domini 1633. A new pulpit was erected in Womborne
church, and a boxe to put in the money collected for ye poore
Item by the consent of the churchwardens, & other parishioners
there was at Mr Ithiel Smarts proper charges, a wainscoat Pew
erected for his wife, the wch he bequeaths to ye Vicaradge for ever
Item in this yeare a Pewter fflagon to serve at the communion
was bought, & a carpet made for the communion Table.
Item a new gate for the churchyard was made this yeare 1633.

John Cartwright }
Robert Bradney } churchwardens

'The old order changeth' – sacking the Parish Clerk 1632.

His next step was to set about remedying defects in the fabric not only of the church, but the vicarage in which he would now live. 'The Vicarage house being much ruined ...', he took steps to get it repaired. The site of this building is not altogether clear and there are no estate maps for that era, so we have to rely on the written word to locate the house. In 1612 the vicarage apparently had a barn and a two-acre garden[7] and there is a terrier dated 1698.[*8] This mentions 'the Vicaridge House which consists of three bays of buildings and a small Brewhouse, the Barn of two bays and a half, the fold yard and two gardens are about a fifth of an acre the two Backsides are about one acre and a half'. If these were all on the same site they must have occupied over two acres. The remainder of the document gives details of the glebe land (land owned by the Church) in other parts of the parish, identifying the boundaries by reference to who owned the land all around it. It was logical at the time but of little help to us in locating the exact site of the Elizabethan vicarage. In 1635 Ithiel writes: 'I give consent that the vicarage should be loaned for the poor after the value of half a yard of land and no more',[†] so it is certainly possible (and in the light of later events, very likely) that the SMART family lived for some time at Trysull, where the church was also in his care. Throughout his time in Wombourne he ensures that the funds for the poor are well managed but it seems unlikely that he was willing to share his house with them – and his wife might have had something to say about the idea.

In the archdeacon's visitation of 1830 the vicarage is described as 'an old building – half brick and half timber; state of: tolerably good. Oubuildings: barn, stable etc. and some smaller tenements in the village – out of repair'. This house, whether the remains of the Elizabethan vicarage about which Ithiel was contemptuous or a partial rebuild, almost certainly stood on glebe land lying to the east of the church, but in 1840 a larger house was built on the south side of School Road, overlooking the church and village. This served until well into the twentieth century when, much too large and too expensive for a late-twentieth century vicar to maintain, it was sold, another more modest clergy house having been built west of the site on which its predecessor stood. The Victorian house became known

* **Glebe, Terrier of 1698**. A terrier is a term specific to the Church of England. It is like a survey or inventory and gives details of glebe land and property. Glebe includes the vicarage, fields and church plus the contents of the church. Income from this belongs to the vicar.

† This sentence is ambiguous but probably can be interpreted as meaning that Ithiel Smart was prepared to rent the vicarage house for a sum of money equivalent to that which he would have got in rent for half a yard of land.

as 'The Old Vicarage' but this in turn was demolished and replaced by houses in what is now called Old Vicarage Close.

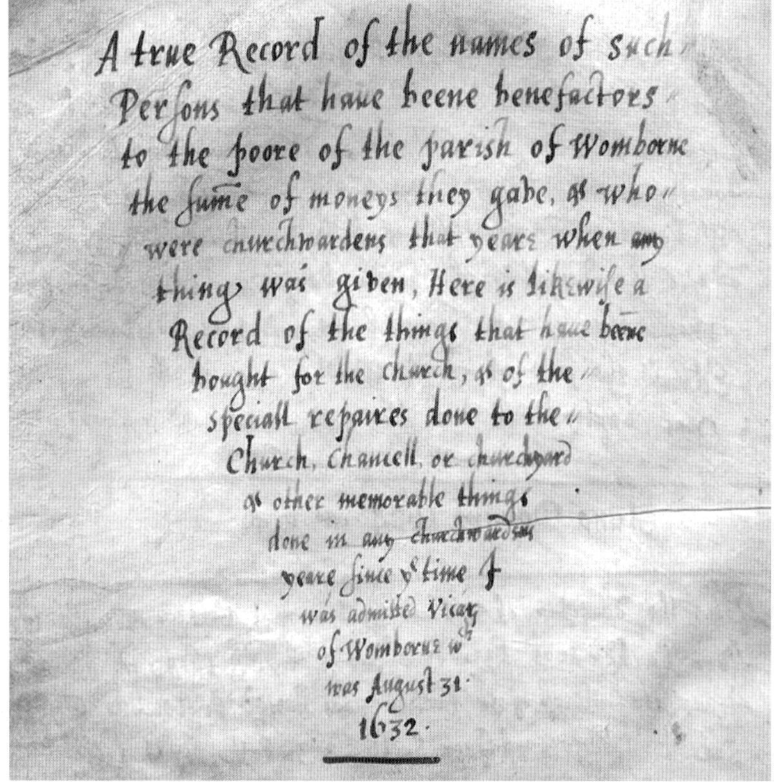

A true Record of the names of such
Persons that have beene benefactors
to the poore of the parish of Womborne
the summe of moneys they gave, as who
were churchwardens that yeare when any
thing was given, Here is likewise a
Record of the things that have beene
bought for the church, as of the
speciall repaires done to the
Church, Chancell, or churchyard
as other memorable things
done in any churchwardens
yeare since ye time I
was admitted Vicar
of Womborne wch
was August 31
1632.

There are regular entries in the records in which Ithiel Smart notes the building and remedial work he has set in hand. He seems to have been a well-organised and fairly hard-nosed man with a good business head who had the equivalent of a five-year plan which would be instantly recognisable by any tycoon today. He was obedient in following the rulings sent down from the bishops; he was apparently zealous in supporting new ideas which sought to sweep away the old ways smelling of popery and introduce more modern ways of conducting church affairs. The year 1633 saw a gate for the churchyard and 'the communion table new rayled'.* Bishop Robert Wright of Lichfield attempted to impose 'a more rigorous conformity & to enforce the railing of altars in response to the metropolitan order of 1634', but Ithiel was ahead of the game. The churchyard was 'new payled about'

* 'new rayled' – wooden railings installed to stop the parishioners actually touching the Communion table.

in 1634, 'the Chancel lathed and seiled and put in sufficient repair'* the next year and 'the church new shingled over' in 1636. Inside work followed: 'the Chancel new painted and adorned with sentences and compartments pews in the north ayle repaired and ...'[9]

The place must have been like a building site for months at a time. Nor were all the changes he made to the church entirely welcome to some parishioners:

> *in 1639 Ithiel SMART the Vicar of Womborn committed an act of enclosure hedging the migrant poor out of access to the circuits of charity and belonging in the local community; he had the church porch gated, railed and bolted in order that 'idle and impotent people might not lodge therein as [they had done] in former times'.*[9]

He had some family life as well, but we know little about it. His wife appears only in the baptismal records of their children as Dorcas 'his wife'. Despite extensive searches in archives all over the country and by using online search engines there is nothing more to found about her: no family name, and even more frustrating, no marriage for the pair. Presumably there must have been a marriage somewhere but the records have been lost. It seems increasingly likely that this took place in London, probably in the City of London, as becomes apparent later in the narrative where various clues indicate this, but there is no proof. Many of the London parish records were lost in the Civil Wars, various fires and in the Blitz of World War II. The pair were certainly married by 1633 because 'there was at Mr. Ithiel Smarts proper charges a wainscoat pew erected for his wife the whc. he bequeaths to the Vicarage for ever'.[10]

They had children too. The following baptisms are all recorded in the Wombourne registers:

1. Ithiel: 20 March 1636
2. Elizabeth: 12 Nov. 1637†
3. Mary: 2 Feb. 1638†

* 'The Chancel lathed and seiled ...' – The chancel is the (almost separate) section at the east end of the church, containing the altar. Maintenance of this is a legal/ecclesiastical quagmire as it has now been declared in some cases to be the responsibility of the laity including the Lord of the Manor. (For a more detailed explanation see Chancel Repair Liability (CLR).) Either way, Ithiel SMART's comments confirm the poor state of the fabric if it needed repair work done to the roof (i.e. laths and ceiling replaced).

† The apparent anomaly in birth dates is because of the confusion caused by when 'the New Year' actually began. Until 1752, when the Gregorian calendar was officially adopted, 25 March (Lady Day) was the first day of the New Year. Most historians overcome this by using a combination of figures e.g. Feb. 1638/39.

4. Dorcas: 24 Feb. 1640
5. Katherine: 6 March 1641
6. Sara: 4 March 1648 (note in the Register says 'to Ithiel SMART and Dorcas his wife vicar pastor of Womborn and Tresle').

Sara 'daughter of Mr. Smart' was buried on 13 December 1649 in Trysull.[11] This is one of the small indications that the family lived there rather than at Wombourne, but it might have been more expedient at the time to bury the child there. Presumably the other four daughters survived; none of their deaths is recorded in either register up to 1652 when he left. There are no marriages for them either, even twenty-five years after their baptismal date. Even if record-keeping was non-existent in most parishes during the war years (and Wombourne was no exception), any event involving one of the vicar's family was surely too important to have been omitted, even if only in retrospect as a late entry. Although five children were born between 1636 and 1641 there is a long gap before the last locally recorded baptism, that of Sara in 1648. There are no SMART children recorded as being baptised, married or buried *locally* between 1641 and 1648. Ithiel SMART was almost certainly away from Wombourne for most, if not all, of these years. This supposition is also given credence by the entry he makes in 1648 when he records the names of those who had been buried during the conflicts. We must wonder who kept the most basic of parish affairs running during those troubled times. Bodies would have been interred by the grave-diggers but some cleric, even itinerant, must have said some hasty words over the bodies before burial; or in such disturbed time was even this ritual omitted or was it too done by the laity?

His children were augmented by other family members. In December 1638 he notes in the records that 'my nephew Nathaniel SMART BA Emmanuel College, began to officiate my cure ...' and when Nathaniel left in July 1640 for Rushall Hall '...his brother Ezekial BA and scholler of Emmanuel ...' stepped (or was fitted) into his shoes. This makes for some confusion. Ithiel's father, Robert SMART, probably had a son called Nathaniel who could have been the 'reader now at Tresle'. However, Nathaniel is identified by Ithiel as his nephew and there is no mention of 'my brother'. There is an Ezekial SMART, singleman, clerk who died in 1650 at Rode in Suffolk where he was vicar. He left no will, but administration of his estate, which included 'ffolios and other books' valued at twenty pounds, three silver spoons, and very little else except money due for tithes, was granted to Nathaniel SMART, so it is reasonable to assume that this was 'his brother Ezekial' – he who came to Wombourne – and they were possibly twins judging by their baptismal dates. Even given the Old Testament names which were given to children in this family it is very difficult to sort out one generation from another. Whichever of the Nathaniel(s) and Ezekial(s) was recruited,[12] the parish got curates of whose allegiance Ithiel was fairly certain and he kept the business in the family. This allowed him more time for his increasing involvement with politics, now inextricably, and fatally, mixed up with ecclesiastical affairs, and everything heading towards a major crisis.

Cahill in an interesting commentary suggests that 'Smart's conformity was partial;[13] following an episcopal visit, Ithiel Smart of Wombourne was presented in April 1639 (before the court at Lichfield) for keeping a fast 'contrary to the king's proclamation ...' Perhaps it was his challenge to any proclamation issued by the King that SMART employed what might otherwise be seen as a Catholic ploy of fasting, but nothing seems to have come of his reprimand. There can be little doubt that he was an undoubted reformist both by upbringing, training and by inclination. The dissenting clergy formed a close, supportive, social circle, including dinner parties together (after the sermon had been heard), and he is known to have been a friend of Richard LEE, the Puritan preacher in Wolverhampton, a town which had not had a Puritan tradition. LEE, in a memorable phrase, described Wolverhampton as a place 'where Rome's snaky brood roosted'. St Peter's Church was a Royal Peculiar and the town had a long connection with Windsor and royalty.

The widening gulf between King Charles I and Parliament must have been felt as sharply in Wombourne as in any other village or town. The division it caused between every layer of society, as well as between friends and families, is well documented. It was undoubtedly felt just as keenly between a Puritan vicar and his congregation, not all of them adherents of the Presbyterian cause. In 1636 William Mulliner was presented (before the local magistrates) for resorting together with other company near to the church at sermon time with feathers in their hats, and 'with bells, drums, taber and pipe making so great a noise that the congregation should scarce hear what was delivered by the minister'.[14] This charge was dismissed with a caution. Everyone wrestled with their conscience, but there is no doubt where Ithiel Smart's allegiance lay. He came from a family of dissenting clergy steeped in Protestant ethics. In 1640 he led the parish (or some of it) in a protest against the King's edict that there should be a 'day of public thanksgiving for peace between England and Scotland'. When the crisis finally erupted into war in 1642 he seems to have deserted the parish at this time. His last entry in the register for six years was on 2 May 1642 in which he detailed the state of 'stocks for the poor'. May Griffiths thinks he left the parish to serve with the Commonwealth army, but this is well-nigh impossible to prove and no evidence found so far supports the idea, attractive though it may be. It seems increasingly likely that he went (back), at least for long stretches at a time, to London. It may be that he wanted to be personally involved as part of the elite Puritan group making the policy decisions; it might have been that he thought it was safer to be in London than in the Staffordshire countryside with sporadic fighting breaking out as the war bands fought over the counties.

Ecclesiastical records say he was 'perhaps sequestered to St. Mary Magdalene, Old Fish St., (City of London) 1642'.[15] It seems ironic that a Presbyterian minister should be in charge of such a named parish. The London Metropolitan Archives have found no reference to him in their indexes to Diocese of London subscription books 1627–48/9 and 1660/1–75,[16] *However, we have found the following reference to Ithiell Smart in the appendix of 'Commonwealth Intruders' in Hennessy's* Novum Repertorium Ecclesiasticum Parochiale Londinense *(1898): Ithell Smart MA appointed 28 Feb 1641/2 Source: Jo[urnal of the] Ho[use of] Co[mmons] vol ii., p983. Within Hennessy's main listing of records of St. Mary Magdalen Old Fish Street, he notes that Mathew Griffith was ejected in 1641–2, and gives the source as 'Comp Book etc'.*[17] Clergy were ejected from their livings for many reasons including refusing to sign the 39 Articles of Faith, as required by law, but was Ithiel a full-time replacement for Mathew Griffith, or was he elsewhere? Unfortunately, records for this period in the archives of the House of Commons were destroyed in the fire of 1834. The House of Lords was dissolved 1642–48, so there were no records at all then from that source.[18]

It seemed that finding SMART in London (if that is where he was) or anywhere else, was a hopeless task. Information seemed to be non-existent, at best very scrappy and discouraging to pursue. A burial is recorded in the BMD Register of St Mary Magdalen, Old Fish Street, London in February 1641 of 'Katherine SMART soiourner' (?sojourner). It might well have been a relative, even the widow of Robert SMART. It could just have been Ithiel's daughter of that name, but as she was baptised in Wombourne on 6 March 1641 it seems unlikely.

There was no obvious link until as late as May 2015. Then a newly transcribed series of BMD Registers for London parishes appeared containing an entry which supports 'the London theory', altering everything. Records of St Mary Magdalen, Old Fish Street, Anno Domini 1644 records a christening (not a baptism) of 'Daniell Smart sonne of Ithiell Smart on 5th May 1644'.

This one brief entry confirms that both Ithiel and Dorcas were in that parish, in London, at that time. They might have made the journey from Wombourne to London for the occasion but that seems unlikely with a new-born baby. They might have decided at some time, perhaps after the fighting had begun, that London was a great deal safer place for the family than Staffordshire. If so, they were correct in

Daniell Smart's christening entry.

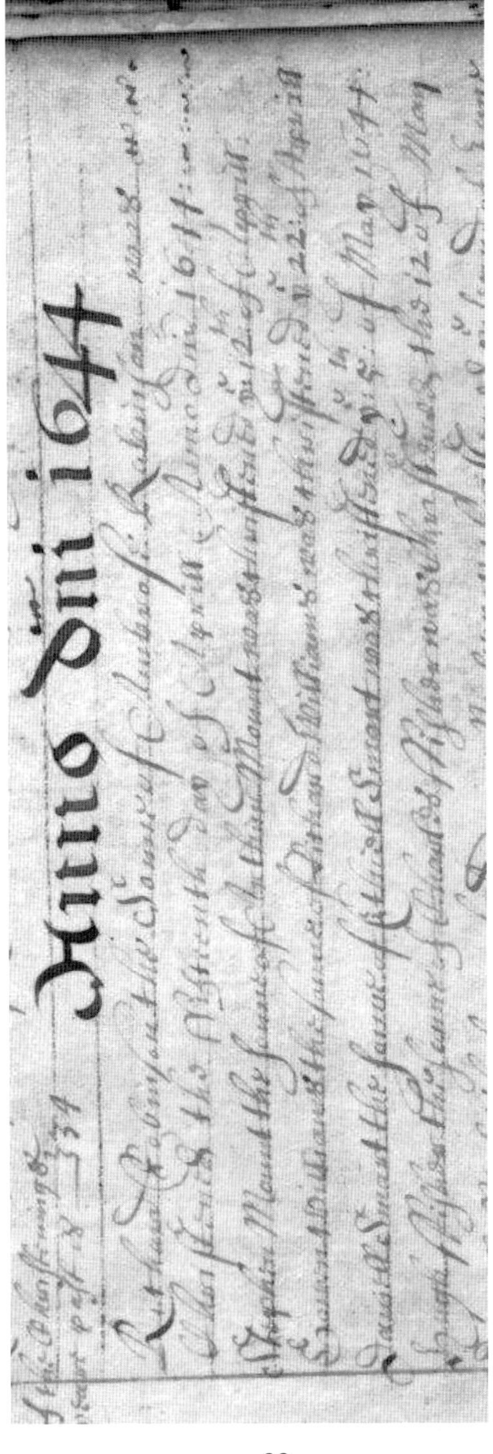

Detail of Daniell Smart's christening entry in the register of St Mary Magdalen, Old Fish Street, City of London 1644.

their thinking. London, despite the risk of plague and other city-centred hazards and diseases, was the political hotbed, but not a battlefield, except of words. Perhaps Dorcas originally came from the City of London, still had family in this parish and the SMART family, including the older children, lived with, or near, her parents or another relative when grandparents or close relatives were able to help in their care. It seems possible that if the older children were in London for some six years they may have remained there, either alive or having died there. No Register of Deaths is available online at the time of writing (May 2015). Since finding Daniell's christening a close scrutiny of the parish records, some of which are now available online, show some entries which look as if they were written by Ithiel SMART, although most appear to be in a different hand. Examination by an expert might confirm or deny this theory.

Ithiel SMART was in London in October 1644 because he was present at the hanging of Francis Pitt, a yeoman of Wolverhampton, aged 65, 'for endeavouring to betray the garrison of Rushall-Hall in the County of Stafford, to the enemy'[19] and wrote an account of the event. In the same year he is described by 'the Committee for Plundered Ministers'[20] as 'a godly and orthodox divine' when it granted him '50 l [£50] pa from the impropriate rectory of Trysull sequestered from Sir Rich. LEVESON, delinquent as his living was but 30 l [£30] pa'.[21] He obviously did not get his money because on 5 Oct 1647 the committee ordered the sheriff, deputy lieutenant and justices of the peace 'to assist Smart to get payment for this augmentation'. History does not show whether or not he ever got his money – probably not. In 1645 he is one of the signatories to a Plea to Parliament in 1645 to establish a Presbyterian government.[22] He was amongst a list of signatories to an appeal of country ministers to the Westminster Assembly in 1648 and is described therein as 'Ithiel Smart, Minister of God's Word at Womborn'.

Later that year he must have returned to Staffordshire. The Wombourne BMD Register for 1642–48 contains the following in his familiar hand: 'The names [*which follow*] of such persons as were buried by reason of the Warrs from the year 1642 to the year of our Lord God 1648'. Record-keeping was chaotic everywhere in times of civil strife, let alone Wombourne in the 1640s, but someone had kept a note of those who had died. SMART was back in the parish by 1648, but his zeal must have been diminished by the horrors of Civil Wars and what had happened in the kingdom. He does note sourly in the Register of 1648/9 that Charles I had been executed, but his own fire appears to have gone out. There are no more glimpses of parish life to be found in the registers.

Dorcas was buried on 3 October 1650 in Trysull,[23] just a year after her baby daughter Sara. (It must be assumed that this was the mother of the family, as most children are identified as 'daughter of …'.) There is no further trace of any of their remaining daughters: no marriages or deaths. The elder son Ithiel went to St John's College Cambridge as a sizar and then, following the family tradition, took Holy Orders, ultimately also becoming vicar of St Helen's, Ashby de la Zouch, Leicestershire. Daniell also disappears without trace from any records found so far, although there is (another?) Daniel in the Venn Register who is supposed to be brother of Ezechial and Nathaniel,[24] but the dates do not fit.

Ithiel resigned his living at Wombourne in 1652 and in July that year became vicar of St Helen's, Ashby de la Zouch, Leics. He remained in this parish until his death in 1661. He did not apparently leave a will so all we have of him at the end is his obituary:

> *Mr. Ithiel SMART, Minister of Ashby, a worthy and faithful servant of God, a famous Divine and a painful Preacher, ye comfort of God's people in his time, departed this life ye 22nd. November and was interred in the Chauncel of our Parrish Church in Ashby ye six and twentieth of November 1661.*[25]

Timeline

?1598 Ithiel SMART probably born in the last years of Elizabeth I who died in 1603
1603 James I (James VI of Scotland) ascended the throne
November 1604 Gunpowder Plot to blow up the Houses of Parliament
1604 Book of Canons (Church laws) issued
1598–1605 Early years were in Northamptonshire during which time Robert SMART, his father, was displaced from his living in Preston Capes. Ithiel's formative years were during James's reign **1603–25**, during which time he went to Cambridge and was ordained.
1625 Charles I ascended the throne
1633 Charles I appointed William LAUD as Archbishop of Canterbury who followed High Anglican practices. Fines for Puritans not attending Anglican Church services.
1634 Charles I, in dire need of money, instituted the Ship Tax. This was applicable to everyone, including those living in inland counties, and resented by all.
1642 First Civil War broke out. Ithiel's entries in the Register cease until 1648.
1643 Lichfield besieged and captured by the Parliamentarians
Oct 1646 Episcopacy formally abolished and the Church remained Presbyterian until the Restoration in 1660.
1648 King Charles I executed on 30 January 1648 in Whitehall, London

1652 Ithiel Smart resigns living of Wombourne and moves to Ashby de la Zouch
1649–60 Oliver Cromwell becomes Lord Protector
1660 King Charles II restored to the throne
1661 Ithiel Smart dies in November 1661

EXCERPTS FROM WOMBOURNE BMD REGISTERS WRITTEN BY ITHIEL SMART

1635 Burial Register
'Thomas RIDER who was struck blind by God's providence being impatient under his cross cut his owne throat'

Notes

1 Revd H. Isham Longden, 'Northampton and Rutland Clergy' no.3: hand-written day book, later pub. 1941.
There is a cautious footnote: 'perhaps identical with the V. of Preston Canes'.
2 All Wills in the Leicestershire County Archives.
3 Longden, Revd. H.I.: *Ibid.*
4 Source CCEd 1540–1835.
5 Source: Liber Cleri LRO B/V/1/62.
6 Now in the care of Stoke on Trent and Staffordshire County Archives.
7 SCH.
8 Stoke on Trent and Staffordshire County Archives: Terrier 1698 Wombourne Glebe land.
9 Revd S. Shaw, *The History and Antiquities of Staffordshire* (London, 1801) vol. ii, p. 217. Quoted in Steve Hindle, 'Destitution, liminality and belonging: the church porch and the politics of settlement in English rural communities *c.*1590–1660', p. 71 in *Social history of Rural Communities*, ed. C. Dyer (Hertfordshire University Press, 2007). All these excerpts taken from the Wombourne Parish Registers.
10 Stafford County Archives: Wombourne BMD Register.
11 Staffordshire County Archives: Trysull BMD Register.
12 See footnote for a family tree.
13 M. J. Cahill, 'The Diocese of Coventry and Lichfield 1603–1642', (PhD Thesis, Warwick University, 2005).
14 LRO, B/V/1/61.
15 M. J. Cahill, PhD Thesis, 2005.
16 LMA ref: MS20, 868/1–3.
17 Comp book: believed to be a ref to Composition Books now in the National Archives at Kew.
18 Email communication from Archivist of the Parliamentary Archives May 2015.
19 British library: Item @ reel 1798:27 (Wing M2699A).
20 Committee for Plundered Ministers. Appointed by the Long Parliament in Dec. 1642 for the purpose of replacing those clergy who were loyal to King Charles I.

21 Bodleian Library MS 323 pp 267, 357, 358.
22 Journal of the House of Lords, p. 718. A1645.
23 BMD Register for Trysull (Tresull).
24 Venn Register.
25 Leicestershire Arch. Soc. papers.

Smith and the Dish

Margaret King

'... Given to the Parish of St. Benedict Biscop, Womborne in 1701 by the Revd. Edward Smith...'

'Oh no,' you may be forgiven for thinking, 'not more eighteenth-century waffle and, please, not another cleric!'

It does not sound like a sparkling start to another chapter about Wombourne's history and it pales even more when it has to be admitted that what we know about the Reverend Edward Smith is – practically nothing. He must, though, have a place amongst the Worthies of Wombourne for he gave the parish one of its greatest treasures.

The Victoria County History, that bible for researchers, is remarkably coy about Edward Smith. It says only he was the son of Edward Smith of Wombourne, which is even less helpful to researchers, although that very lack of knowledge is comforting. If those who compile the bible cannot find out more there is very little indeed to be found.

The Clergy of the Church of England Database, ignored at one's peril when searching out clergy because it is an invaluable source of information, has equally little to say about him. There are seventeen entries for Ordinands called Edward SMITH, but only one who fits into the time frame and has a Staffordshire connection. This is the Edward Smith who received his BA at Magdalen College Oxford and his MA at Magdalene College Cambridge between 1663 and 1669. He was ordained in Lichfield Cathedral in 1672 and then became vicar of Penn for just one year. Once again, there is no more about him: no information as to where he went after Penn and this assumes that we even have the right Edward Smith.

There was a family called Smith who owned considerable amounts of property in and around Wombourne in the late seventeenth century and there were Catholic recusants called Smith whose names appear in earlier records, but nothing to connect to our man. Edward Smith is not a name which leaps off a page to greet you.

The Portuguese silver dish was given by the Revd Edward Smith to the parish of Wombourne in 1701.

If the man is difficult to trace it is of little real importance to the story, except for the irritation of NOT knowing about him. The importance lies not in *who* he was but *what* he did.

Edward Smith gave the 'Parish of Womborne' a treasure; a most astonishing gift of huge importance, not just to the village, but to the wider world. This was 'the Womborne Dish' and we now know far more about this than we do about its donor, thanks to research by Museum curators and other scholars. Their conclusions were:

> At the centre of this small silver dish is a caravel, the sailing vessel that was helping to make Portugal the most successful European trading nation in the early 16th century, when it was made in the capital, Lisbon. Portuguese trade routes and networks expanded rapidly in the 15th century through the journeys of exploration of Prince Henry the Navigator (1394–1460), Bartolomeu Dias (1451–1500) and others. By the 16th century, this small country's presence had extended to Africa, South America, India, Sri Lanka and the Far East, and Lisbon became for a time the key financial

> and trading centre for Europe. Caravels contributed to this success because they were more effective at sailing windward, allowing ships to leave the safety of coastal waters and head out into the Atlantic.
>
> With its highly symbolic sailing ship and its powerful decoration, a frieze of triangular shapes resembling a blazing sun, interspersed with floral motifs, the dish is an excellent example of Portuguese silver from the early 16th century. It has no Portuguese marks, but does have London hallmarks for 1606. It is in fact a rare surviving example of the practice of striking London hallmarks on imported foreign plate, to allow it to be traded legitimately in the City of London. An almost identical dish, now in the Museu Nacional de Arte Antiga, Lisbon, also has London hallmarks, for 1610. It is not known how the two dishes reached Britain, but the Wombourne dish is next heard of when, in 1701, it was given by the Revd Edward Smith to the church of St Benedict Biscop in Wombourne, Staffordshire. Smith had an inscription engraved around the rim on the back of the dish, recording his gift as 'for ye use of ye Communion table of Ye Parish Church of Womborne'.

They found that the dish was made in Portugal, sometime between 1510 and 1520. There is another very similar dish in a museum in Portugal, but we have no idea how 'ours' came to England. It was traditionally known in the parish as 'the Armada Dish' and it is possible that it was booty acquired from that great victory for the English (and disaster for the Spanish), but we do not know this. What is indisputable is that it was hallmarked by the Assay Office in London in 1606, for the marks can be clearly read. It was not apparently unusual at the time to have foreign silver re-hallmarked in this way so that it could be legally traded here. Who owned it and where it was kept for the next hundred years is also unknown, but Edward Smith must have acquired it from somewhere, or even inherited it, before having it engraved around the back rim with the words '*for ye use of ye Communion table of Ye Parish Church of Womborne*' before he gave it to the parish.

It was used in Wombourne church, usually as an alms dish, on high feast days and special occasions, until the responsibility of owning and storing safely such a valuable item became a burden to the vicar and churchwardens. The risk of theft was very real and it was almost impossible to insure. The market value lay in what it would have brought when put up for sale and that course was very unlikely, even if 'selling the family silver' would have been a considerable help to the parish finances.

The dish was discretely put into safe keeping for a considerable time and reappeared in 2014 in London for a short time on exhibition in the Wallace Collection. It is now on long loan in the Barber Institute, University of Birmingham. Here it may be seen and admired by far more people than ever caught a glimpse of it at Christmas or Easter on the altar of the church to whom it still belongs.

Perry, Powell and 'Prentices!

Margaret King

A single entry in a tax ledger of 1710 is Richard Powell's only claim to fame. He would hardly even have been noticed there, except for his address in Wombourne.

Most of the people in this book make our acquaintance in the conventional manner. Their biographer starts with their parents, the infant's birth or baptism and proceeds through their life story, whether worthy or otherwise, usually signing off with their death. They have a beginning and an end.

Not so Richard POWELL. He arrives almost by accident, ready-made, probably aged about 12 years old and then is gone again. We get just the one swift glimpse of him: no beginning and no end. Not much of a story about him then, but that one brief glimpse is what makes him such a challenge.

Research on family and local history is usually done for personal reasons. People seek for details of their own family and often to try to construct a family tree. Parish records of baptisms, marriages and deaths, and census returns are the basic tools of the trade and often provide the information required. With luck (and a bit of help sometimes) the searcher may well succeed in tracing their relatives back into the late eighteenth century. Some are less lucky and get stuck at what is known as a 'brick wall' very early on, although even brick walls can be demolished – sometimes. Increasingly, much research is done, very successfully, solely by using the internet, where there are vast amounts of information becoming accessible on a daily basis. For more detailed and advanced work, as well as for accuracy, a visit to the appropriate archive to look at original documents is still necessary and rewarding, if time-consuming.

Richard Powell and his family came out of obscurity from the page of a magazine. In all fairness it was a history magazine. Jeremy Goldsmith was discussing a new source of information recently released – Apprenticeship Records – and used a page, presumably chosen at random, to illustrate his article.

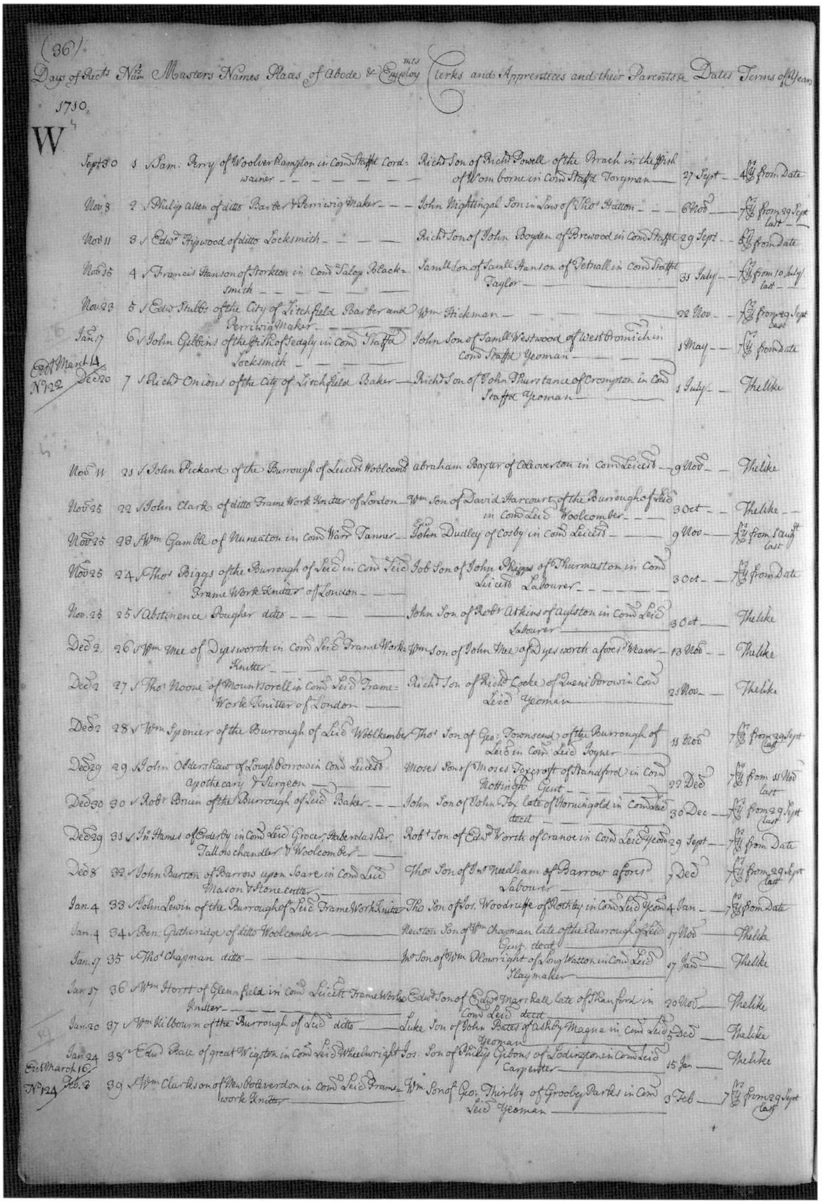

(36)

1710

W

Days of Recpt	Num	Masters Names Places of Abode & Employmts	Clerks and Apprentices and their Parents &c	Dates	Terms of Years
Sept 30	1	Sam: Perry of Woolverhampton in Com Staff Cordwainer	Richd Son of Richd Powell of the Brach in the Parish of Wombourne in Com Staff Yeoman	27 Sept	4 Yrs from Date
Nov 8	2	Philip Allen of ditto Barber & Perriwig Maker	John Nightingal Son in Law of Thos Hatton	6 Nov	7 Yrs from 29 Sept last
Nov 11	3	Edwd Fipwood of ditto Locksmith	Richd Son of John Boyden of Brewood in Com Staff	29 Sept	5 Yrs from Date
Nov 15	4	Francis Hanson of Storkton in Com Salop Blacksmith	Saml Son of Saml Hanson of Petnall in Com Staff Taylor	31 July	7 Yrs from 10 July last
Nov 23	5	Edw Stubbs of the City of Litchfield Barber and Perriwig Maker	Wm Hickman	22 Nov	7 Yrs from 29 Sept last
Jan 17	6	John Gibbins of the Parish of Sedgly in Com Staff Locksmith	John Son of Saml Westwood of West Bromich in Com Staff Yeoman	1 May	7 Yrs from Date
Entd March 14 No 122 Dec 20	7	Richd Onions of the City of Litchfield Baker	Richd Son of John Thurstance of Crompton in Com Staff Yeoman	1 July	The like
Nov 11	21	John Pickard of the Burrough of Leicestr Woolcomb	Abraham Baxter of Coleoverton in Com Leicestr	9 Nov	The like
Nov 25	22	John Clark of ditto Frame Work Knitter of London	Wm Son of David Harcourt of the Burrough of Leic in Com Leic Woolcomber	30 Oct	The like
Nov 25	23	Wm Gamble of Nuneaton in Com Warr Tanner	John Dudley of Cosby in Com Leicestr	9 Nov	7 Yrs from 1 Augt last
Nov 25	24	Thos Biggs of the Burrough of Leic in Com Leic Frame Work Knitter of London	Job Son of John Briggs of Thurmaston in Com Leicestr Labourer	30 Oct	7 Yrs from Date
Nov 26	25	Abstinence Pougher ditto	John Son of Robt Atkins of Aylston in Com Leic Labourer	30 Oct	The like
Dec 2	26	Wm Mee of Dysworth in Com Leic Frame Work Knitter	Wm Son of John Mee of Dysworth aforesd Weaver	13 Nov	The like
Dec 2	27	Thos Moore of Mountsorell in Com Leic Frame Work Knitter of London	Richd Son of Richd Cooke of Queniborow in Com Leic Yeoman	25 Nov	The like
Dec 2	28	Wm Spencer of the Burrough of Leic Woolcomber	Thos Son of Geo: Townsend of the Burrough of Leic in Com Leic Joyner	11 Nov	7 Yrs from 29 Sept
Dec 29	29	John Alderslaw of Lough Borrow in Com Leicestr Apothecary & Surgeon	Moses Son of Moses Foxcroft of Standford in Com Notingh Gent	22 Dec	7 Yrs from 11 Nov last
Dec 30	30	Robt Bown of the Burrough of Leic Baker	John Son of John Fox late of Horningold in Com Leic decd	30 Dec	7 Yrs from 29 Sept last
Dec 29	31	Jn Hames of Enderby in Com Leic Grocer, Haberdasher, Tallowchandler & Woolcomber	Robt Son of Edw Worth of Cranoe in Com Leic Yeom	29 Sept	7 Yrs from Date
Dec 8	32	John Barton of Barrow upon Soare in Com Leic Mason & Stonecutter	Thos Son of Jno Needham of Barrow aforesd Labourer	7 Dec	7 Yrs from 29 Sept last
Jan 4	33	John Lewin of the Burrough of Leic Frame Work Knitter	Tho Son of Jos. Woodruffe of Rothley in Com Leic Yeom	4 Jan	7 Yrs from Date
Jan 4	34	Ben: Gutheridge of ditto Woolcomber	Newton Son of Wm Chapman late of the Burrough of Leic Gent decd	17 Nov	The like
Jan 17	35	Thos Chapman ditto	Jno Son of Wm Plowright of Long Watton in Com Leic Slaymaker	17 Jan	The like
Jan 17	36	Wm Hortt of Glennfield in Com Leicestr Frame Work Knitter	Edwd Son of Edwd Marshall late of Shanford in Com Leic decd	20 Nov	The like
Jan 20	37	Wm Kilbourn of the Burrough of Leic ditto	Luke Son of John Bates of Ashby Magna in Com Leic Yeoman	5 Dec	The like
Jan 24	38	Edw Brace of great Wigston in Com Leic Wheelwright	Jos. Son of Philip Gibbons of Lodington in Com Leic Carpenter	15 Jan	The like
Entd March 16 No 124 Feb 2	39	Wm Clarkson of New Botteverdon in Com Leic Frame work Knitter	Wm Son of Geo: Thirlby of Grooby Parks in Com Leic Yeoman	3 Feb	7 Yrs from 29 Sept last

The 1710 Apprenticeship Indenture for Richard Powell.

Summs and Values given or contracted for and Duty's (36)

Memorials of Indentures Articles	Collectors	Subcollectors	£50 or under	6d Duty	above £50	12d Duty
Common Indr & Countery		Unett (George) to Gilbert Walmesley	5	02 6		
The like			12	06		
The like			2	01		
The like			3 05	01 7½		
The like			13	06 6		
The like			5	02 6		
The like		Porter (Robt) to Ditto.	10	05		
		£	50 05	1 05 1½		
The like	Ward (John) at Leicester		1	6		
The like			4	02		
The like			15	07 6		
The like			4	02		
The like			5	02 6		
The like			2 10	01 3		
The like			4 10	02 3		
The like			3	01 6		
The like			49	1 04 6		
The like			10	05		
The like			10	05		
The like			2 10	01 3		
The like			7	03 6		
The like			9	04 6		
The like			6	03		
The like			3 10	01 9		
The like			5	02 6		
The like			4	02		
The like			3	01 6		
		£	148	3 14		

50

Apprenticeship is a long-standing method of teaching of a trade, craft or skill to a child by a master in the same trade or profession. Historically it was formalised by an agreement, often called an indenture, between the parent or guardian of the child and the new master. The parent or guardian paid a sum of money (a premium) to the master in return for the tuition and the master kept the child housed, clothed and fed until the apprenticeship ended, usually after seven years, and the youngster could earn a living. The 1563 Statute of Apprenticeship made it compulsory for anyone wishing to enter a trade to take up an apprenticeship and this was taxed at sixpence for every pound of the premium and one shilling for every pound above fifty pounds per annum. The exception to this was in the case of paupers. The parish, who had to pay for a pauper child's upkeep, off-loaded this liability, at no cost to themselves, as soon as the child was deemed able to work. Some new masters may have been kind to their new charges. Many more, particularly after the Industrial Revolution led to the setting-up of factories and to mechanisation, simply saw pauper children as a source of expendable cheap labour and justly earned a reputation for brutality. They ran sweatshops at very little cost to themselves except the food and basic necessities of life which would keep the child alive. If the child did not survive the long hours of work and the sometimes brutal living conditions there were plenty to replace it.

In 1709 the government, as chronically short of money as governments usually are, but particularly so when the expenses of the war with France (the War of the Spanish Succession) were increasing, found a new way to raise a bit of cash. Someone had the bright idea of making parents pay to register their children's indentures, leading to the Stamp Act of 1709. This put a tax on indentures and required that all were registered centrally.

This gave rise to *The UK Register of Duties paid for Apprenticeship Indentures 1710–1811*, to give the full title.

In the County Register for October 1710, at the top of page 96, appears the entry for Richard Powell from Wombourn. Other apprentices come from Brewood, Stafford, 'Tetnall' and West Bromwich. No addresses are given; it is apparently enough to identify them just by the bare name of their town or village.

Why then is Richard singled out as from 'The Brach in the Psh of Wombourn'?

Wombourne was a small, insignificant village of little importance compared with the county town of Stafford, or of West Bromwich or even of 'Tetnall'. Why does the clerk give him, *and him alone*, an address and identify him as coming from a small lane called 'The Brach'?

Addresses in documents of this time are rarer than hen's teeth and this, combined with the pleasure of finding someone from Wombourne, sparked off a new piece of research.

Powell is a fairly common name in and around the counties bordering Wales, so disentangling one family from another is very difficult. Entries in the baptism registers are kept to the barest minimum around the early eighteenth century: they often consist only of the surname and Christian names of the child, his father and sometimes the mother, usually described as 'wife of ...'. The same Christian names appear time after time. Details of burials are even briefer, so how is a poor researcher to distinguish one buried William Powell from another?

Searching the local parish registers from about 1670 to 1730 produced four POWELL families, the heads of the families being:

1. William, born about 1670
2. Daniel, born about 1675, married in 1695/6
3. Richard, born before 1670
4. Thomas, born before 1680

Their dates of birth are guesses, based on the ages at which their children were baptised, as we have no places of origin for them. There are another thirty-nine people whose names appear in various registers and documents around those dates and who may, or may not, be related.

It became obvious that the four families were probably related and that the wives were all of child-bearing age. They were producing children all around the same time and some of these had the same Christian name.

1. William POWELL and Jane had four children, Thomas, Daniel, William and Jane. All were baptised in Wombourne between 1691 and 1699. No marriage details for the parents have been found.
2. Daniel POWELL married Mary GRICE in St Bartholomew's, Penn: '*both of ye.Psh.Of Wombourne were married with licence the sixteenth day of Janry.1695*', so we know that both were living locally at that time. (There is a Mary GRICE, daughter of William GRICE, whose baptism is recorded in the Register of Penkridge on 26 February 1679, but this does not really help.) They have four children, Elizabeth, John, Ralph and Hannah, who were baptised in Wombourne between 1697 and 1704.
3. Richd. POWELL (the Forgeman* and father of the apprentice Richd.) must have been born before 1670, but no marriage to

* **Forgeman** Wombourn has had many mills, often powered by water. There was a considerable amount of metalworking being carried out throughout the Smestow valley in the eighteenth century and items of every sort were shaped on forges of all sizes.

Mary appears in the local registers, so we do not know her maiden name. They may have married outside the area or not have been married at all.

There are seven known children in this family. John, born 1691, and Thomas, born 1697, were baptised in Wombourne, as was Mary in 1700 and the following three children no.5 Sarah in 1704, no.6 William in 1706 and no.7 Ralph in 1709. So six of their names appear in Wombourne baptismal records between 1691 and 1709, but Richard's is not amongst them.

Richd. was most likely to have been about 12 to 14 years old when he went as apprentice[**] to Sam. Perry, the Wolverhampton cordwainer, so he was probably born around 1695/6. (No trace is to be found of Sam PERRY of Wolverhampton, the cordwainer,[†] despite searches in the Wolverhampton Archives.) The rationale for this is that if he had been born before John he would have been too old at 19 for apprenticeship. After 1700 he would have been too young.

It is also interesting to note that his apprenticeship was only for four years, not the more usual seven years. Apprenticeship to shoemakers was considered to be at the 'lower end' of the social scale. However, it may simply reflect the cost to his father of paying the premium and the stamp duty even if the former were paid by instalment, which was not uncommon. The outlay was considerable, even if Richd. the Forgeman was

At this period a forgeman was a specific title, implying a skilled metalworker who usually had others working under him. Within these four families many of the children have the same names and the assumption must be, for lack of evidence found so far, that there were probably four brothers and their families (or even a father and three sons) all living somewhere in the parish, possibly all working together. It is possible that all lived in the Bratch, but the construction of Brindley's canal in the 1770s altered the conformation of the land here and removed evidence of earlier dwellings. The families probably worked at Heath Mill. This was an important industrial site using power generated by the combined forces of the Tene and Wom Brooks which join forces just before the site of the mill.

** **Apprenticeship and adolescence** In the second half of the seventeenth century it became common practice to send sons and daughters away from home as apprentices around the age of puberty.

Children from all levels of society from labourers to the yeoman class as well as clergy were treated thus. Nobility and the landed gentry had their own methods of dealing with adolescent children, including sending them away to school even in the early 1700s.

Ref: Diary of Ralph Josselin, b.1617. Vicar of Earl's Colne, Essex 1641–1683.

† **Cordwainer** A shoemaker, specifically of soft fine leather shoes (as distinct from a cobbler, who mended shoes).

slightly better off than the other members of the clan, who may have worked for him. Certainly he is the only one whose occupation is noted in the church register and this is confirmed by the apprenticeship register entry. Angus Dunphy[1] says 'in the 1690s the Powells operated the forge' (at Heath Mill, south-west of Wombourne), but does not quote the authority for this.

There is a burial entry on 18 May 1823 in Wombourne for a Richard POWELL, but no indication as to whether this is 'our' father or son.

4. Thomas POWELL, born before 1680. There is no marriage entry in Wombourne or other local registers for him and wife (?) Anne, but there are six children born between 1700 and 1708, all of whom were baptised in Wombourne.

   Letters of Administration were granted on 18 May 1739 to Phoebe POWELL, widow of Thomas POWELL *'late of the said parish of Wombourn'*. Unfortunately there are no details given about his occupation, and the names of the two persons mentioned as executors, John DUMBLETON of Dudley, Maltster, and Edward PRICE of Dudley, Nailor, are of little help. Phoebe POWELL makes her mark but the two executors sign their names, the latter as 'Edward PRICE senior'.

So the family history ends there, unsatisfactorily for those who like a tidy solution to a detective story.

It is, however, typical of this sort of research. The brief appearance of the POWELL families is only interesting because of the detail given about Richd., the young apprentice cordwainer. The families flare into the history of Wombourne like sparks from the forge and are as quickly gone again.

Note

1 Angus Dunphy, *The Smestow: Wolverhampton's River* (Black Country Society, 2012)

Oh, Happy Day!

Margaret King

The Marriage Register of St Benedict Biscop contains the following entry:

'7 July 1834. ***Richard TOMLINSON****, bachelor to* ***Mary JONES,*** *spinster, by Banns.*
Witness: ***Thomas FLAVEL'S*** *X mark'*

In the space reserved for the signature or mark of the second witness is written:
'Happy Guest's X mark'

And if you don't believe it you may check for yourself, but you shall be the one to decide whether anyone whose name is mentioned (or not) is Worthy.

MARRIAGES solemnized in the Parish of [illegible]
in the County of Stafford in the Year 1834

Richard Tomlinson of this Parish
Bachelor
and Mary Jones of this Parish
Spinster
were married in this Church by Banns with Consent of
this seventh Day of
July in the Year One thousand eight hundred and thirty four
By me James Bevan Curate
This Marriage was solemnized between us { Richd. Tomlinson's + Mark
Mary Jones' X Mark
In the Presence of { Thomas Flavel's + Mark
Happy Guest's + Mark
No. 412.

The Policemen of Wombourne

David Taylor

On 6 November 1849 Robert Holmes was buried in Wombourne church; he was aged 35 and had died of consumption (called tuberculosis today). He had resigned as a police officer on 31 October 1849, although it is difficult to believe he had been as active in the role in the final months of his life as the police authorities usually required. Ten days later, William J. Heale, the vicar of Wombourne and Trysull, William Chinner, who owned the Wodehouse estate, William M. Sparrow, who lived at the Heath House and was an ironmaster, and John Hill, a Wombourne landowner and farmer, sent a letter to the magistrates of Staffordshire asking that pay owed to Robert's widow Esther should be paid quickly and she should be considered for a grant because she and her four young children were 'un-provided for'. As a police officer's wife Esther would have been expected to have actively supported her husband in his role, which meant, amongst other things, not taking on paid employment. On 21 December 1849 William J. Heale sent a letter to John Hayes Hatton, the Chief Constable of Staffordshire, asking for his help with the magistrates in this matter.[1] Heale says that Robert Holmes had been the police officer in Wombourne for 'the last few years'. So he may have been part of the founding of the Staffordshire Police Force. Baptism records indicate that he was in the village as a police officer for at least three years. His son Eli was baptised on 31 May 1846, followed by a daughter, Anna Jane, on 30 April 1848, and another son, Robert John, on 25 November 1849. Robert John was born nineteen days after his father was buried, and he himself was buried on 27 January 1850.

A county-wide police force was created with the formation of the Staffordshire Constabulary in October 1842 under the provisions of the County Police Act of 1839. Modern policing in Staffordshire grew out of the system of parish constables and watch committees which mainly operated on a parish basis up to the early part of the nineteenth century. In the 1830s there began a series of more or less co-ordinated

The Staffordshire police uniform, along with all others in the country, originally consisted of a swallow-tail coat and top hat.This changed in the 1860s when the frock coat and pillbox (or kepi) hat were introduced, as seen in this picture.

attempts to reform and update the system to meet the requirements of growing towns and cities and new theories on the organisation of local government. The first major piece of national legislation was the Municipal Corporations Act of 1835 which contained provisions for the establishment of police forces in the 178 Royal Boroughs, but the process had begun earlier in some areas.[2] Borough police forces were established for Walsall in 1832, Newcastle in 1834, Wolverhampton in 1837 and Tamworth and Stafford in 1840. The first county force had three districts: the Mining District which covered Bilston, Willenhall, West Bromwich, Wednesbury, Smethwick and Handsworth; the Pottery District which covered Tunstall, Burslem, Hanley, Stoke, Fenton and Longton, and the Rural District which covered the rest of the county, including Wombourne. This police force operated throughout the nineteenth century, with various amendments incorporating or creating separate borough police forces as the perceived policing needs demanded.[3] For example, the Lichfield force was created in 1856 but rejoined the county force in 1889. The Stafford force consolidated with the county force in February 1858. Hanley borough force was formed in 1870. In 1910 the county force that covered the Potteries were merged with the Hanley borough force to create the Stoke-on-Trent City Police.

Not everyone was in favour of this reform or of the model to be adopted. Magistrates and Members of Parliament argued that a centralised and permanent police force was 'unnecessary', 'un-English', 'unjust' and 'expensive'; they also noted that it would undermine their social control of their locality.[4] Furthermore the general distrust of a body of men patrolling the streets at the bidding of the central and local authorities ran deep. The image of an armed and uniformed force, styled on the military and using violence to suppress demonstrations, is graphically provided by T. Woollaston's memoirs from his service in the police force of Newcastle under Lyme. During the riots in July 1842 in Newcastle under Lyme he recalls that whilst delivering prisoners to the local gaol the police and soldiers were attacked by a mob. In regaining control of the situation the 'gang of prisoners showed great unwillingness to proceed' through the mob, they 'were only prevailed to do so by urgent and repeated blows from the truncheons of the Specials, which were unsparingly used both upon prisoners and all who came within their reach'.[5] How effective the police force were in dealing with riotous behaviour was questioned, for example in the case when George Bibb charged John Potts, both special constables, with assault at an election in Walsall in February 1841. The mayor commented that 'he was very sorry to say that many of the constables were drunk on that day, and that instead of endeavouring to keep the peace they assisted to break it'.[6] 'More or less serious rioting' occurred at the 1874 elections in Wednesbury, Stoke and Wolverhampton when 'the police were at time more or less overpowered', according to Chief Constable W. Congrieve in his report to the Quarter Sessions.[7]

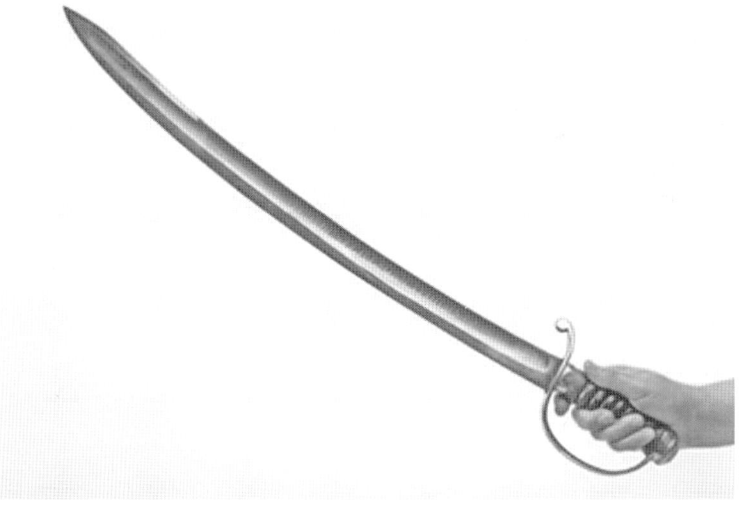

The sword was given to a police officer after the Chartist revolt of 1842. Rioters were intending to destroy local property but they passed the town by. It was thought to be due to Mayor W U Lester and head police officer Isaac Cottril, who had gathered a force of 800 special constables and more volunteers to join the force.

A riot following the Cardiff parliamentary election in 1886 resulted in a number of complaints being made to the Cardiff Watch Committee. One of them was from Councillor Vaughan, who reported that he said to Mr Hemingway, the Head (Chief) Constable, that 'if you want to stop [the trouble] withdraw your men, or you will provoke a riot'. Mr Hemingway is reported as replying: 'If you speak to me again I'll knock you down.' Councillor Vaughan provided further details of police violence against 'orderly and respectable' men and reported that Mr Hemingway was 'shouting like a maniac "Drive them off the street"'.[8] This degree of mistrust and lack of control the Watch Committee had over the activities of their Chief Constable was caused by the ill-defined provisions of the 1835 Municipal Corporation and the 1856 County Police Acts.[9]

This distrust was felt most by the working class, many of whom thought that the new police forces would target them because there existed amongst the higher classes a fear of their 'disorder, impropriety and legal aberration'.[10] However, this distrust was echoed in the middle class as well, but for different reasons. The ratepayers of the parish of Haughton sent a petition stating their concerns about an 'armed and uniformed force' subject only to a chief constable's command rather than the 'supreme power of the state'; that the Chief Constable would be almost beyond the control of the local ratepayers, and yet the ratepayers would have to pay the bill; and that magistrates in court would not know how much they could rely on the statements of police constables who they did not personally know.[11] The general competence of policemen was also questioned because they were 'taken from a class not very competent to judge what are reasonable grounds for a charge of felony'.[12]

However, despite much suspicion and negative perceptions, the role of a permanent, professional and national police force became thoroughly established in England during the nineteenth century.[13] This chapter will look at two different groups of men who served in the county police force, those who served in Wombourne and those who came from Wombourne. Unfortunately, detailed service records have not survived to us showing where men served, so that information is gleaned from the 1841 to 1901 census records and the county police registers of police, essentially a record of joining, promotion and leaving the force for most of the nineteenth century.[14] These sources allow a picture to be built up of the police officers of Wombourne.

Part of the process used to establish local confidence in the police force was the enforcement of strict discipline on the police officers themselves. Regulations stated that the police constable 'will devote the whole of his time and abilities to the service'; he is to 'especially avoid drinking and smoking in public houses he is most likely to come into contact with' on a professional basis and that he is to 'execute his duty with good temper and discretion' with no unnecessary violence and not to provoke or offend with his language.[15] It also meant that they were essentially on duty twenty-four hours a day, seven days a week.

Breaches of this code of conduct and the punishments given were recorded in a disciplinary book. Some of the men in the sample can only be described as 'repeat offenders' and not necessarily with the same types of offences. Richard Biddulph and Josiah Hammond both had ten recorded 'disciplinaries', in careers that lasted twenty and twenty-six years respectively, an average of one disciplinary every two years. John Dobson, with thirty-two years' service, incurred eight disciplinaries, an average of one every four years. William Enoch served for six years but incurred seven disciplinaries. However, thirteen of the twenty-nine in the sample had no recorded disciplinaries. Whilst some of these men spent only a few months in the force, Thomas Thorpe served for thirty years and Samuel Price for twenty-eight. These were exemplary performances given the standards applied. Punishments were ranked as fining, de-ranking and dismissal, but with de-ranking least used.[16]

In total there are sixty-six recorded disciplinaries, with an extremely wide range of different causes. The most common involved alcohol, usually cited as drunk on duty, which accounted for fourteen. The punishment for disciplinaries involving alcohol seemed to be very variable. John Tucker after his second disciplinary was discharged, whilst Richard Biddulph after his eighth was merely fined five shillings. It may be that the length of service was also an important determinant of the punishment; John Tucker had been in the force for five months whereas Richard Biddulph had twenty years' service, and four months later he retired. Was there an element of protecting the pension of Richard Biddulph? Conversely, the more senior the rank the higher the standard and the greater the punishment seemed to be. Joseph Ainsworth, when he was a sergeant in October 1885, was charged with 'drunk off duty' for which he was fined ten shillings.

More minor disciplinaries included being absent from or late arriving for a conference, recorded six times; not properly dressed, recorded twice, and 'neglecting their diary', recorded three times. It should be noted that in the days before mobile telephones, two-way radios and other electronic means of communication the conference points and times were essential means of keeping police officers in touch with each whilst on the beat. Officers on the beat had to be at specified locations at specified times, these locations and times being co-ordinated so that officers on the beat would regularly meet other officers. This allowed messages to be passed on and sergeants to meet with their constables. If a conference was missed this raised the alarm that something untoward had happened to the constable. Altogether these accounted for seventeen per cent of the total number of disciplinaries, not an excessive proportion of the total. Furthermore, the 'usual suspects' appear in the record for all of these disciplinaries; Josiah Hammond, Richard Biddulph and William George Morris for three each and Joseph Ainsworth and Thomas Sidney Ledbury for the other two. The impression we are left with is that some police officers were not up to the standards expected, but if they had the service record to support them they were merely fined and occasionally cautioned.

However, some of the disciplinaries seemed to be more important and involved serious breaches of duty. Richard Biddulph seems to have been a frequent offender. His first recorded disciplinary was on 6 September 1862 when he allowed 'a prisoner to escape' for which he was demoted to police constable second class. Then on 10 January 1864 he was charged with 'neglecting to execute a warrant' and punished with the relatively large fine of ten shillings. This was followed four months later on 26 April 1864 with a charge of 'neglecting duty in a case of rape'; his punishment was to be 'removed', which meant that he was moved to another station. Finally, his last breach of duty was 'improperly causing a prisoner to be detained for an undue time' on 18 August 1873, for which he was fined seven shillings and six pence.

Josiah Hammond, even though he is recorded with a similar number of disciplinaries as Richard Biddulph, seem to be of a different character. There appears to be only one serious breach of duty when he was charged on 28 February 1875 with 'neglecting to take sufficiently prompt measures to apprehend offenders', for which he was reprimanded. What exactly the measures were that he did not take is not clear. Similarly with Thomas Sidney Ledbury, his charge of 'gross neglect of duty' on 3 December 1879 received the punishment of demotion from sergeant to police constable first class. This was a little over two years after the promotion which took him twelve years to procure.

As well as a duty to the public there was a duty to brother officers and to their superiors. Joseph Ainsworth was charged on 25 January 1886 with 'neglecting to visit men on duty and the station at night', for which he was reprimanded. Presumably, as absent without leave is not cited, he did not miss a shift. Therefore, by not showing concern for the men under his command by visiting them and the station at night he was not performing his duty. Josiah Hammond on 9 February 1884 was accused of two charges: firstly of 'disloyal conduct towards a brother officer', for which he was fined the substantial amount of thirty shillings. As a sergeant this would be almost a full week's wage of thirty-five shillings and sixpence. The second charge was 'showing strong animus against a constable' for which he was transferred to the Mining District. Whatever the details of the case, it is apparent that the force protected junior officers from unfair behaviour of their seniors. However, due respect was expected, as Thomas Sidney Ledbury found out on 26 May 1872 when he was charged with 'insubordination in making unbecoming remarks on the conduct of his superior officer', for which he was fined five shillings.

What appears to be the relatively closed world of the police force is shown by the fact that in the 1891 census William Foden is lodged in the police station with Thomas Sidney Ledbury, wife Mary Ann Ledbury and a general servant Eliza Simmonds.[17] With this level of contact it is not surprising that tensions within a police station could on occasions reach boiling point. Joseph Ainsworth and Samuel Bellings were charged with 'quarrelling in their station' on 27 December 1870. Both were to be removed from Darlaston station. Perhaps they were good officers, and the quarrelling was merely verbal. In contrast, Robert Williams on 1 August 1877, after just over a year in the force, was charged with 'drunk on duty and fighting', for which he was dismissed with immediate effect. It is not clear whether he was fighting another officer or a member of the public, but the combination of his age, the alcohol and the fighting clearly required the police force to apply the ultimate sanction. Interestingly, he appeared to know what the verdict was going to be, because it is noted that he deserted before the punishment could be announced.

Supporting brother officers was very important to the police, and where serious breaches were identified the repercussions were high. William Enoch on 1 October 1878 along with James Banton was charged with 'not going to assist a constable who had just been violently assaulted and from whom a prisoner had been rescued'. On being found guilty the punishment was a severe reprimand. Four years later he was subject to a similar disciplinary on 14 June 1882; however, this must have been more serious because the charge was 'cowardice and failing to assist a comrade when in danger during an affray'. Again there was another police officer charged at the same time, Edward Handcock, and both were dismissed with effect from 15 June 1882. It was also important for the police to gain the trust of the public; therefore, 'unbecoming behaviour to a member of the public' was also of concern to the senior management of the police force. The police constable's regulations stipulated that he had to 'execute his duty with good temper and discretion', with no 'unnecessary violence', and his language had to be such as 'not to provoke or offend'.[18] When William Enoch was charged with 'unbecoming conduct in the witness box' on 24 October 1881 his punishment was to

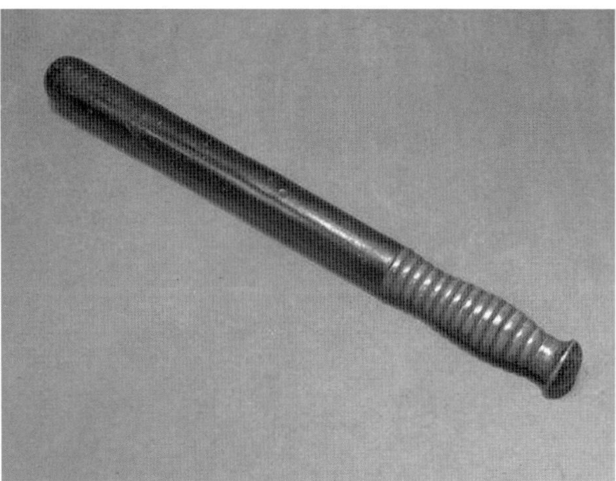

At 17 inches long and 1.5 inches wide, made from ebonised solid mahogany, this is a typical example of a Victorian police truncheon. They were freely brandished as a threat when situations were at risk of becoming violent.

be reprimanded and to forfeit his special duty pay. On 24 July 1878 Thomas Hickman was charged with 'spending upwards of two hours in a public house when on duty and giving false evidence before the magistrates' and was dismissed. The charge of being in a public house whilst on duty would normally be a fine of about five shillings, so the dismissal must have been because of the false evidence before magistrates. When Richard Biddulph was charged with 'striking a drunken man with a stick' on 14 February 1863 he was both fined five shillings and severely reprimanded. John Dobson was charged with 'indiscretion and incivility in entering a premises to serve a summons' on 6 June 1871, for which he was reprimanded. It would be interesting to know more of the background of this case, but whatever the circumstances it is clear that discretion and civility were expected when dealing with members of the public. Thomas Sidney Ledbury also seemed to overstep the mark when he was charged with 'unduly searching premises and making a disingenuous reply to the complaint' on 9 May 1880. For his conduct he was fined ten shillings, about a third of his week's wage at the time.

As in today's police force there were some obvious 'bad eggs' and when they were identified it appears the punishment was substantial. Samuel Wood, who had served for fourteen years as a police constable first class, was charged with 'unlawfully taking and detaining a watch and endeavouring to conceal the fact'. He was dismissed on 15 July 1881. Incidentally, there appears to be no evidence for a prosecution in the local courts for the theft; was it deemed sufficient to have dismissed him?

Maintaining the reputation and standards of the police was an obvious and important objective in all of these charges. At the same time there appears to be recognition of past good service in the setting of punishments. Perhaps the best example of this is the case of Joseph Ainsworth who on 7 November 1874 was charged with 'quarrelling with his wife to the scandal of the force'. His punishment was to be 'removed at his own cost', that is moved to another station. The addition of 'at his own cost' appears to be very unusual; perhaps it was thought that the opportunity to start afresh in another station should not be seen as too lenient a punishment by ensuring that there was a financial implication as well.

It is noteworthy that disciplinaries were not always a hindrance to a policeman's career. Two men in the sample achieved the rank of superintendent. Samuel Price incurred no disciplinary entries in the records in twenty-eight years in the force. However, Joseph Ainsworth also became a superintendent even though his record included six disciplinaries over thirty-six years in the force. These included quarrelling with a brother officer, scandalising the force by quarrelling with his wife, being drunk off duty and neglecting to visit his men on night duty. Presumably he was seen as being good at his job and past indiscretions or mistakes were not weighed against him.

If bad behaviour and breaches of regulations were punished, then the opposite was encouraged. Police officers were expected to be vigilant at all times, and were rewarded for being so. There were eight recorded commendations, three for one person and one each for four people. Thomas Thorpe received three commendations, on 23 November 1881, 1 January 1883 and 16 January 1890. On two occasions he received a reward of ten shillings, approximately a third of his weekly wage, and on the third occasion he received fifteen shillings, half of his weekly wage. These sums of money would have been appreciated by him, and hopefully his family. Certainly he would appear to have been what would be described as a sober man, because he is one of the thirteen men who did not have a disciplinary record. His first commendation was for 'arresting one of two fowl stealers when on night duty'. His second was for 'courageous conduct when assaulted by poachers', which he received along with Police Constable John Goode. The third was for 'prompt detecting of pigeon stealers' along with Police Sergeant William Upton. In all three commendations he is based in the Rural District which may explain the nature of the occasions, involving fowl, poaching and pigeons. Certainly fowl and poaching indicates stealing for food, which would have been more easily done in the country compared to the towns and cities of Staffordshire. Pigeon-stealing is a little more ambiguous; pigeons were kept for food, but breeding for display and racing was, and remains, a popular Black Country pastime.

Personnel of Burslem Police Force line up for an official group photograph at the end of the nineteenth century. Notice the uniforms of the late Victorian era. After Queen Victoria's death in 1901 the uniforms changed slightly, blue shirt and tie, helmet and jacket replacing the cap and smock coat.

The other commendations went to Thomas Sidney Ledbury on 1 April 1882, Joseph Ainsworth on 20 October 1871, William George Morris on 4 April 1883 and Henry Collier on 13 February 1893. Three of these names are familiar to us from the disciplinary ledger discussed earlier. Thomas Sidney Ledbury was commended for 'tact and coolness in dealing with a gang of poachers'. Was he developing into a highly effective police officer after the earlier part of his career when he seemed to be marked with insubordination and a cavalier approach to the duties of a police officer? On such scanty information, it is difficult to draw a firm conclusion.

The following men received commendations early in their careers. Joseph Ainsworth was commended for 'detecting gaming in a public house'; this was relatively early in his career as he joined the force on 1 May 1867. An ability to investigate potential and actual crimes is perhaps shown in the commendation, the implication being that the gaming was not obvious and required some detective work. He finished his career as a superintendent, only two ranks below that of chief constable for the county. William George Morris's commendation was for 'detecting boatmen stealing coal from a boat'; he had joined the police force in 1879. Henry Collier was commended for 'creditable detection of two thieves and a receiver of their stolen goods'. Along with Inspector William Bakewell, he had joined the force on 13 August

1889. Whether there was a deliberate attempt by the authorities to reward long service it is difficult to determine, but there is a clear pattern with four of the five men who received a commendation doing so in their fourth or fifth year of service, the only exception being Thomas Sidney Ledbury.

The commendations show two important requirements of the police force. Firstly, there was the identification and resolving of crimes, for example 'detecting gaming' and the 'detection of two thieves and a receiver'. Secondly, and perhaps more importantly for the citizens of Staffordshire, was the deterrence and immediate presence at the scene of a crime that walking the beat provided, for example 'arresting one of two fowl stealers' and 'prompt detecting of pigeon stealers'. Another aspect to policing that developed as the century progressed was that of the implementation of local government responsibilities such as lighting and paving and weight and measures. These responsibilities do not show up in the commendations.[19]

Finally on the commendations, what can they tell us about crime in Wombourne in the nineteenth century? For the whole of the period from 1874 to 1915 that is covered by this analysis there is only one mention of Wombourne as the scene of a crime with a commendation. That occurred on 26 August 1915, when Police Constable Charles Scott detected a poacher and was rewarded with five shillings. Perhaps Wombourne was a relatively law-abiding parish, but the mostly rural environment made poaching and animal thefts the obvious local crime. Certainly, on Sunday, 31 July 1862 Police Constable Dobson, having been alerted by Joseph Bullock that one of his fowls was missing, found himself in pursuit of two fowl thieves. Within half a mile Dobson and Bullock caught up with Joseph Moseley and Henry Powney, with Powney in possession of the fowl. At the police court Moseley said he knew nothing about the fowl, and Powney said he picked it up thinking it was his brother-in-law's (Moseley). Given that Moseley, Powney and Dobson are all recorded in the 1861 census as living in the centre of the village, it is likely that they all knew each other. Bullock is recorded as living in Blacklay, which would explain the half a mile chase.[20] In addition, it was presumably Police Constable Dobson who dealt with the cases of illegal fishing at the Woodhouse by William Tonks and Thomas Walford and two counts of poaching by William Thomas that went to the courts in September 1863.

The authorities preferred new recruits who had some experience of life. Twenty-one of the men were appointed when they were between nineteen and twenty-two; the eldest was Joseph Carter, who was twenty-seven years and one month, followed by Samuel Wood, aged twenty-six years and eight months and then Samuel Price who was twenty-six years. Prior to appointment to the force, fourteen of the twenty-nine described themselves as labourers, the next most common occupation was shoemaker for three men and blacksmith for two. The remaining occupations included tailor, stocktaker in the iron trade, wheelwright, gardener, shingler and brewer's cellarman. There appears to be no difference in the breadth of occupations depending upon the home parish of the man, so it is unlikely that there was a bias in recruitment. However, it is notable that none are described as agricultural labourers. In Wombourne this was the most common occupation throughout much of the nineteenth century, so one would have expected to see it represented in this sample. Further investigation of census records shows that the term 'labourer' covered any person who described themselves as agricultural labourers or labourers of different types. This all fits well with Carolyn Steedman's findings that labouring was the dominant category of pre-recruitment occupation, and that failure in another occupation, such as shoemaking, or an assessment of comparative benefits, was a usual reason for recruitment.[21] The pre-recruitment employment of the men reflected the employment opportunities of the county at large, and this is clearly seen in this sample.[22] For those who rose through the ranks, background appeared to have little impact on the ultimate rank achieved. The two men who became superintendents, Samuel Price and Joseph Ainsworth, recorded their occupation previous to entering the force as labourer. This is in sharp contrast to Carolyn Steedman's findings, which showed that it was rare for a police constable, especially from a labouring background, to attain officer rank.[23]

Other information collected at the date of appointment to the force included height: the average height was just over five feet nine inches. There were three men recorded as being six feet or more, the tallest being John Biddle who was six feet and one inch. The shortest was James Shotton at five feet six inches. All except one, Samuel Price, was recorded as single, which we might expect for a population that was mainly aged about twenty-one. Again this is very much in line with Carolyn Steedman's findings.[24] Nine of the men gave references, mainly from local people, the most notable being the Reverend W. J. Heale, the vicar of Wombourne and Trysull. Seven men state that they have previous service, meaning either in the armed services or with another police force. Josiah Hammond, who was born in Tuddenham in West Suffolk, had served six months with the East Suffolk police. No information is provided on why he moved to Staffordshire, but Steedman comments that there were many examples of men using the police force as a method of making changes or transitions in their lives. Three men served in their local volunteer regiments. Thomas Ledbury served with the 1st Battalion 22nd Regiment of Foot, but it is noted that he served for 'nil years and nil days', which might mean that he did no more than sign up. Perhaps he was rejected for some reason. Henry Collier served with the 2nd Grenadier Guards for three years from 1886 and then was on the army reserve. The seventh man was Charles Rowley who served for 106 days with the Royal Garrison Artillery just before the First World War. He rejoined the army in 1915, and was killed later that year.

The analysis of the recruitment records of the Wombourne sample shows that there were no cases of local men being posted to Wombourne after their training. This somewhat undermines the argument that local knowledge was important in recruitment or in making a 'successful policeman'.[25] If local knowledge was important, we might expect to see at least one Wombourne man being based in Wombourne. Perhaps there merely had to be an appreciation of locality, rather than an intimate knowledge? Indeed, Carolyn Steedman notes that 'most county forces ... stationed recruits ... some distance from their most recent home and birthplace'.[26] This would be an obvious move to avoid accusations of favouritism or undue influence.

Table 1: *Proportions of Men Leaving The Force*

Category	Wombourne Sample (Numbers)	Wombourne Sample (% of all leavers)	Steedman Extract (% of Turnover in 1880)*
Resignation	7	25	70
Dismissal	9	32	27
Pension	8	29	10
Other	4	14	n/a
Total	28	100	n/a

* Percentages do not add to 100 due to the imprecise presentation of the data. What is important here is the relative importance of each category. The higher level of Wombourne sample pensioned and other leavers perhaps reflects the extended period over which the sample is drawn, compared to taking a small number of individual year's intakes. The similar proportions of dismissals probably reflects a continuing level of 'harsh discipline' from 1880 to 1914.

Sixteen of the twenty-eight Wombourne sample were traced in the censuses after they left the force. Other than those who retired, they went on to a variety of different occupations, perhaps because, as Carolyn Steedman suggests, the 'drilling and smartening up' from police training allowed the men to move on to another more lucrative occupation.[27] James Shotton became an engine fitter, but also worked as a general labourer. Richard Biddulph went on to become a publican, which was an interesting choice because he left the force as a result of ill health from diabetes. Eli Garner went on to become a bookkeeper, whilst William George Morris became a watchman in a brewery. Dismissal from the police force was not always a negative impact on their future careers. In some cases they went on to make good careers, although it should be noted that many of these were men who worked for themselves. So it is possible that the lack of a good reference from the police force did push men into a certain type of occupation – those who could work on their own account. Samuel Wood, who was dismissed for unlawfully taking a watch in 1881, eventually became a farmer with his sons and daughter. William Enoch, who was dismissed in 1882 for cowardice, became at different times a life assurance agent and a dealer in furniture. John Potter and Charles Deans went back to their previous occupations of tailor and bootmaker respectively. John Tucker, who was dismissed in 1863 for being drunk, worked as a labourer in a glass works for a while and eventually ended up in Kinver as a jobbing gardener.

We have an insight into the ending of a policeman's career through the superannuation, or pension, fund records that have survived. Obviously this will only cover those men who stayed in the force for a long time. The shortest period of service was twenty-one years by Richard Biddulph and the longest was thirty-six years by Joseph Ainsworth. The average for the eight men who are recorded as receiving a pension up to 1915 was almost twenty-nine years of service. The average age at retirement was 51 years. Receiving a pension, at a time when most people had no such luxury available, would have been a major attraction in recruitment to the police force for some of the men. Working men's choices at the time were to work until they died or became dependent upon either their family or the New Poor Law Union. The opportunity to retire in their fifties on a pension would have been valuable, even if it was not immediately appreciated by the new recruit.[28] The extent of the benefit is seen by analysing the reasons given for retiring. There were four men, with an average age of 53, who reached thirty years of service and expressed a desire to retire. Another four men, with an average age of 50, retired due to being unfit for service. The reasons were wide-ranging: there were cases of diabetes, 'extensive valvular disease of the heart from repeated attacks of rheumatic fever', contracted tendons of the forearm and 'chronic rheumatism'. On average they were retired for eleven years before they died, whilst those who reached thirty years of service lived for another twenty-one years.

The information provided in the superannuation records may explain some of the behaviour of Richard Biddulph. His diabetes may have been partially responsible for some of the disciplinaries he received. His being 'drunk on duty' could have been a misinterpretation of some of the symptoms of diabetes. Further, and perhaps more telling, many of his disciplinaries were due to neglecting his duty in some way. For example, he was late attending a conference, allowed a prisoner to escape, neglected to execute a warrant, neglected his duty in a case of rape, patrolled a different route to the one he was ordered to follow and 'improperly' caused 'a prisoner to be detained for an undue time'. So many unusual disciplinaries may indicate an underlying medical condition which caused lack of concentration. His last disciplinary on 28 January 1879 was for being drunk on duty and was followed less than three months later with being granted early retirement due to diabetes on 15 April 1879.

James Crump was born in Wombourne on 10 October 1840 to Henry and Hannah Crump, an agricultural labourer and his wife, and baptised in Saint Benedict Biscop on 8 November 1840. They had moved into the village sometime between 1823 and 1827 from Trysull, a typical move for an agricultural family as they looked for work. James was the last of eight children, who were born between 1821 and 1840, a child every two or three years. He was three years younger than his next oldest sibling, Hannah. When James was born his eldest brother, John, was a nailer, a common occupation in the village, and his second oldest brother was an agricultural labourer, the other common occupation in the village. Unlike the typical life cycle for the village, many of his brothers and sisters stayed in the village until into their twenties and thirties. John left sometime before his thirtieth birthday, but he returned unmarried in his forties to live with his widowed mother. Charles lived his whole life in the village, eventually marrying Elizabeth Pyatt in 1864 when he was 23. Richard was over 25 when he left the village but was back by 1881 when he was in his fifties. Thomas and Sarah Crump left the village in their late teens or early twenties, whilst Hannah and James left the village when they were in their twenties. They appear to be a close-knit family, particularly attached to the village; some of those who moved away were buried in the village cemetery. Hannah, his sister, was buried at the age of 33 in 1870.

James lived with his parents first in Bullmeadow and then later in Over Street, now Church Road, in the middle of the village. This tended to incline him to agricultural labouring, as it was on his doorstep. Perhaps he had ambitions, or a desire to do something more than work as an agricultural labourer, like his father, for all his life. He decided to do something different and on 1 January 1862, the start of a new year, he began a new occupation by joining the Staffordshire County police force. He was 5 feet 10 inches, single with grey eyes, light-brown hair and a fair complexion. He was recommended by Frederick Turton Sparrow, an ironmaster living in Trysull, and five others. James had obviously put some effort into making sure he would be accepted by the police force. It is likely he would have done his initial training at Castle Church police barracks before being assigned to a station as a police constable third class. He was not a model police constable, but he was not the worst, his only disciplinary record being for 'drunk and asleep on duty' on 11 April 1862. Typically, to make an example on an impressionable young police constable, he was fined seven shillings and sixpence, between a quarter and a third of his weekly wage, and cautioned.

He was sent for his first posting to Stoke-on-Trent, a large town dominated by the potteries industry. As a police constable he would have been assigned a beat which he would be expected to patrol diligently. It was a matter of importance that each street on the beat was visited during the duty session.[29] An inspection of the Rural District on 11 August 1862 by General Cartwright, the Government Inspector of Police Forces, was 'satisfied with their appearance and efficiency'. [30] The Staffordshire Police Force was well run and fulfilling its public duties and no doubt James Crump would have contributed to this efficiency.

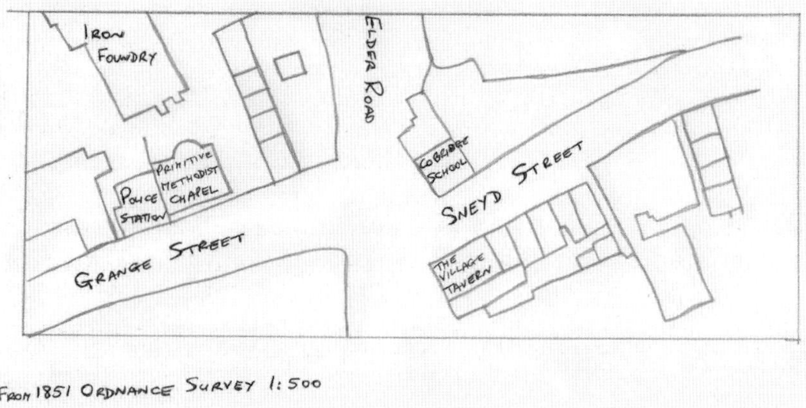

Hand-drawn map by David Taylor from 1851 Ordnance Survey 1:500.

His duty on 18 August 1862 probably began as they all did, arriving at the police station parade, finding the beat he was allotted to and who he might be working with, if anyone. There would have been a briefing on important matters to note for the duty and conference times and points confirmed. Then it was a case of walking the beat. The beat went without incident, none that were noted, and finished at nine p. m. James met Thomas Wells, a fellow officer and a regular drinking partner, and a friend of Wells called Thomas Turner by the Black Boy public house, just off the Eldon Road in the Cobridge area of the Potteries, at about five to midnight. Cobridge is a village between Burslem and Hanley along the A50 or the Waterloo Road as it is known at this point. It was a patchwork of houses, potteries and open fields. They decided to go on to the Village Tavern Inn less than a quarter of a mile away, where they arrived at about twenty past midnight.

In the Village Tavern Inn Wells and Crump were treated to an ale by Turner. When Wells finished his drink he left the inn to begin his beat, but Crump and Turner remained. According to John Platt, the landlord, they left the inn at about one a.m.

Near to the public house three local potters, Absalom Simpson, aged 32, John Hughes, aged 42, and John Wardle, the oldest at 45, were talking about dog racing. They all lived in Sneyd Street in Hanley only half a mile from the inn on the other side of the A50. John Platt confirmed that they had been in his inn as well, and had had a pint each of his ale. When James reached them he ordered them to move, in accordance with regulations not to 'allow such numbers to collect as will obstruct the free passage of the streets'.[31] Simpson took exception and refused. Hannah Field was disturbed by a noise coming from the direction of the Village Tavern Inn, she opened a window and reported hearing an altercation taking place with raised voices and then the sound of a scuffle, which was followed by thuds and finally the sound of running feet. According to Hannah Field the whole incident took about ten minutes.

A little after one o'clock in the morning John Platt went outside to close the shutters of the Village Tavern Inn. He heard groans and went to investigate. He found a man lying on the floor holding the back of his head and bleeding 'fearfully'. He helped the man to his feet and sat him on nearby garden rails. John Platt recognised the voice of James Crump when he replied to John's questions about what had happened to him. John Platt took James into his house and laid him on some pillows. He then went out to find Thomas Wells, but failing that went to the local police station and reported the incident to the duty officer, Isaac Bailey. Isaac went to the Village Tavern Inn, saw James Crump and called for extra help, then he looked for James's staff, which he found near to where he was lying when John Platt found him. When extra officers arrived they took James Crump to the Hanover Street police station, from where Superintendent Samuel Cole ordered that Mr Fairman, a surgeon, should be brought to attend to him. Mr Fairman arranged for James to be taken to the North Staffordshire Infirmary.

The police immediately began a search for the three men, who were quickly found and taken to the infirmary on 20 August, with witnesses, to be identified by James Crump as his assailants. James Crump positively identified all three men as his assailants and, adding weight to his identification, positively identified a fourth man, Millward, as not being involved at all. After this Simpson, Hughes and Wardle were charged with assaulting Crump whilst in the execution of his duty. Wardle and Hughes made statements saying that Simpson had assaulted Crump, whilst they stood a little way off. The doctors considered the injury, a compound fracture of the skull, to be life-threatening.

Crump survived until 25 September, when he died in the evening. He was 21 years old and had been a police constable for seven months.

The jury at the coroner's hearing held on Saturday, 27 September returned a verdict of 'aggravated manslaughter'. At the magistrates' hearing on the following Wednesday, 1 October, Simpson, Hughes and Wardle were accused of murder, but the defence counsel argued for manslaughter. The magistrates agreed with the prosecution that there was enough evidence to commit the three for trial on the capital offence of wilful murder. The trial took place at the Stafford Assizes on 5 December 1862. The case for the prosecution was straightforward, that Crump had positively identified the three men who had assaulted him, that the wounds were consistent with a prolonged and considered assault and that as a policeman he was reasonably executing his duty.

The defence, as would be expected in a trial where the charge, if proven, called for the death penalty, explored many avenues such as whether Crump was of a quarrelsome nature or was drunk when leaving the Village Tavern Inn. However, the defence rested on two major points. Firstly, that at different times before he died James Crump gave different descriptions of his principal assailant, Absalom Simpson. The first, and presumed to be the most accurate, was very different from Simpson, to the extent that they were like 'night from day'. The second description was while Crump was lying in a hospital bed dying.

The second point was the exact interpretation of the charge – murder of a police officer executing his duty. This had to be wilful, that is the defendants set out to kill James Crump and that they knew he was a police officer. The evidence presented by many people strongly suggested that it was not wilful and that there was no 'malice aforethought'. Further, it was not clear that James Crump was executing his duty. He was not in uniform, he was not known to the assailants as a policeman and he had not made it clear that he was a policeman executing his duty.

The defence for Hughes and Wardle further rested on the evidence of many of the witnesses, expert and factual, who contended that only one man was responsible for the assault, and that clearly it was not either Hughes or Wardle. Murder required an active participation, not just attendance at the scene. In this the defence was assisted by the successful plea for all three defendants to be tried in the same trial. In this way they could not be called to give evidence against each other.

The judge's summing-up stated that 'the jury would have difficulty in saying that any of the prisoners had been guilty of wilful murder, because there were grave doubts as to whether Crump was in the due execution of his duty'; therefore the case was only of manslaughter. The judge went on to say that Crump did appear to be 'officious' in ordering the three prisoners to move on. Further, there did not appear to be a plan to assault Crump, or that all three were actively involved. Finally, he outlined some technical issues with the way the evidence had been gathered and used by the prosecution.

The jury retired to deliberate. After a short period they returned to the court to announce all three were 'not guilty' to the charge. Simpson, Hughes and Wardle were discharged and the court rose at a little after 21:00.[32]

Absalom Simpson moved to Leeds with his wife Mary and his children Margaret, Absalom and Taylor. His daughter Lucy was born there in 1865. Two years later they were back in Stoke and in 1871 they were in Etruria in Hanley where he worked as a potter. He seems to have continued to move frequently: in 1881 he was in Swinton in Rotherham and in 1891 he was in Kidsgrove in Staffordshire.

Both John Wardle and John Hughes disappeared from official records after the trial. Perhaps they died; as potters their life expectancy was relatively short at 46.5 years.[33] Another option is that they moved out of the area, as Simpson did, and changed their names. This was easily done in the nineteenth century when it was very difficult to verify a person's name and history. Or perhaps it is part of the difficulties of identifying a specific John Wardle or John Hughes from a list of similarly named individuals living in the same urban location.

James Crump was buried in Wombourne cemetery near to Saint Benedict Biscop's Church on Monday 30 September 1862. In the year to 29 September 1861 there were thirty-two attempted murders, eight manslaughters and nine murders reported in the county of Staffordshire. Assaults on police constables were regular and frequent occurrences. [34]

In many ways the police officers of Wombourne in the nineteenth century appear very similar to those of the twentieth and twenty-first century. The technology and equipment has changed and some of the extended moral probity has been relaxed, especially for wives, but the people themselves are very recognisable. Some had their own problems, some coped well with the pressures, some progressed within the police force and others stayed only for a short while. The regular pay, the clothes and boot allowance, the subsidised housing and the pension scheme compensated for the difficulties and restrictions of the life.

Bibliography

An exceedingly good book on the subject, giving an overview and providing lots of detail is Emsley, Clive, *The Great British Bobby – A history of British policing from the 18th century to the present* (London: Quercus, 2009)

For a more extensive detailed analysis of the men of the police force in a critical period of their development see

Steedman, Carolyn, *Policing The Victorian Community – The Formation of English Provincial Police Forces 1856–1880* (London: Routledge & Kegan Paul, 1984)

Notes

1 Staffordshire Record Office Q/SB 1850 A/8.
2 Carolyn Steedman, *Policing The Victorian Community: The Formation Of English Provincial Police Forces 1856–1880* (Routledge & Kegan Paul, London, 1984), pp.13–16.
3 Steedman, p.26.
4 Steedman, p.18.
5 Thomas Woollaston, *Police Experiences and Reminiscences of an Official Life* (Reprint: Berkswich History Society, Stafford, 2007)
6 *Wolverhampton Chronicle*, 17 February 1841, p.1.
7 1874 Election Report to the Quarter Sessions, April 1874 (Staffordshire Record Office C/PC/viii/2/2).
8 'The Disturbances At Cardiff', *The Times*, Thursday, July 15, 1886, issue 31812, p.5.
9 Steedman, p.47.
10 Steedman, pp.63 and 67.
11 Petition of the Ratepayers of the Parish of Haughton, 1844 (Staffordshire Record Office QSB 1844E).
12 Steedman, p.31.
13 Steedman, p.63.
14 The following Staffordshire County Council archive records have been extensively used: C/PC/1/6/1 First County Force Register 1842 to 1863; C/PC/1/6/2 Second County Force Register 1863 to 1894; C/PC/12/1/29/3 Third County Force Register 1894 to 1935; C/PC/1/6/3 Superannuation Book 1842 to 1928; C/PC/15/1/1 Defaulter's Register 1857 to 1886; C/PC/12/1/37/1 Commendations 1874 to 1920;
15 Regulations for the Conduct of Constables in the Staffordshire Police Force 1859 (William Salt Library, 7/139/00).
16 Steedman, p.108.
17 England and Wales Census, 1891.Class RG 12, parish: Wombourne, county Staffordshire.
18 Regulations for the Conduct of Constables in the Staffordshire Police Force 1859 (William Salt Library, 7/139/00).
19 Steedman, p.14.
20 *Wolverhampton Chronicle*, 3 September 1862.
21 Steedman, pp.70, 71 and 81.
22 Steedman, p.77.
23 Steedman, p.106.
24 Steedman, p.80.
25 Steedman, p.102.
26 Steedman, p.117.
27 Steedman, p.85.

28 Steedman, p.111.
29 Regulations for the Conduct of Constables in the Staffordshire Police Force 1859 (William Salt Library, 7/139/00).
30 *Wolverhampton Chronicle*, 20 August 1862.
31 Regulations for the Conduct of Constables in the Staffordshire Police Force 1859 (William Salt Library,7/139/00).
32 All details from the trial are from the *Birmingham Daily Post*, 6 December 1862, issue 1361.
33 Marguerite Dupree, *Family Structure in the Staffordshire Potteries 1840–1880* (Clarendon Press, Oxford, 1995), p.85.
34 Steedman, p.67.

Sam Redfern and the Mount Pleasant Inn

David Taylor

In 1901 Wombourne was a village of less than 1,900 people mainly occupied on the land, in domestic service or in a variety of tertiary occupations. However, in this very down-to-earth community one person's occupation stood out – Sam Redfern, comedian. Who was he? What was he doing in Wombourne?

Who was Sam Redfern?

Sam Redfern, or Samuel Redfern Philips to give him his full name, was born in Birmingham in 1849. By the time he was 18 he was appearing at the Walsall People's Music Hall with his act describing him as a 'nigger'. In the mid-nineteenth century in British music hall this meant a white man who blacked up as an African – that is, they covered their faces and hands with black greasepaint. They sang, danced, and told jokes and comic stories. (Some people might remember *The Black and White Minstrel Show* on television.) Redfern was on the programme at the music hall for the first week in August 1867, which included Mr and Mrs Harry Ridyard (duettists), Mr Alf George (comedian), and Miss Nellie Glover (singer).[1]

The following week he was at the Leith Music Hall, just outside Edinburgh, where he shared the bill with Mr Norman Thomson (baritone). It may be that he didn't go down well here because a review of the show tells us that Norman Thomson, an 'old favourite, was greeted with a cordial welcome and was much applauded', but there is no mention of Sam Redfern.[2] Notices of this type were sent to *The Era*, a London-based newspaper specialising in the theatre and music hall, by anyone local, and described as 'their own correspondents', although they would often be the performers or managers of the theatres. Sam must have had some success in Leith because the following year he was back in the town, this time at the Royal Music

Hall. He is again described as a 'nigger', but this time he has 'much comic talent' and was 'warmly applauded'.[3]

In 1870 he was playing at the Dudley People's Music Hall as a 'Negro' comedian and dancer and received 'a very flattering reception',[4] whilst at the Walsall Alexandra Music Hall he was 'the old favourite'.[5] Wherever he went he was appreciated and his act included enough variety to appeal to a wide audience: comedy has already been mentioned, and his dancing was described as 'peculiar' and 'extremely clever'.[6] Tastes change; in line with many 'nigger' acts, what we would see today as unpalatable caricatures and stereotypes were accepted as 'curious eccentricities'.[7] He also 'delighted the audiences with his comic sayings', monologues based on his Negro character which allowed him to adopt the nickname 'Black Philosopher'.[8] He obviously wanted to broaden his act because in May 1872 he placed a notice in *The Era* to find a partner to work with him, an 'instrumentalist preferred'. [9] By June he had teamed up with Will Harris and they announced themselves as 'original and versatile negro artistes' who were playing at the Prince of Wales Concert Hall, Wolverhampton.[10] The duets with Will Harris lasted about a year because in May 1873 he was back to working solo as an 'old and favourite negroist'.[11]

The year 1874 saw Sam at the Royal Music Hall, Holborn, apparently his first performance in London, the biggest and hardest audience to reach in Britain.[12] It was here that he started to move away from song and dance and develop his 'Black Philosopher' routines. The review notes that Sam has 'plenty to say for himself' and 'undertakes to prove how... the fair sex spring from mulberry trees': apparently it has something to do with 'silk becomes ladies'.[13] Later in the year, at Newcastle upon Tyne's Victoria and Oxford Music Halls, he was described as amusing all by 'his smart and pointed witticisms'.[14] Back in London at the Marylebone Music Hall, his act is described as 'cynical observations'.[15] In 1877 he delivered a 'droll discourse about "Woman"' as well as his song 'Happy Sam' and a dance routine.[16] By 1886 his act was described as containing 'blunt ditties'.[17] In 1899 he performed 'his discourses on things in general with his usual gusto'.[18] Perhaps the tone of his act can be gauged by the satirical column in the magazine *Judy: The Conservative Comic* which was toying with the idea that music-hall artistes would deliver Sunday-afternoon lectures: the one delivered by Sam Redfern would be titled 'The Morals of the Music-Hall'.[19] Innuendo, both subtle and unsubtle, was rife in music-hall acts as the following description of Sam Redfern's act, which he performed to tremendous applause, shows: 'with a greasy wink at Box B, he chortled "I like to get spooning with a scrumptious little girl, in the moonlight, lovely moonlight."'[20]

Success bred imitation, which took many different forms. There was identity theft, as a letter to the editor of *The Era* on 18 August 1872 highlighted.[21]

Twenty-three years later a more sincere form of flattery was practised, and showed that Sam Redfern remained very popular, when Harry Tate at the Concert Hall in Birmingham included an imitation of Sam in his repertoire.[22] As with all successful performers Sam made it look easy: he 'had an easy way of ingratiating himself into the favour of his hearers, and his songs were loudly applauded'.[23] Sam's catchphrases were being widely used, especially 'another excuse for a tiddley', meaning a reason for having a drink.[24] At the turn of the century, the public showed that he was still very much appreciated; following shows at Birmingham's Gaiety and Empire Music Halls, the reviewer said that 'the exceeding funny patter with which Sam Redfern always manages to entertain his audience was a feature of the programme last evening, and Sam received a very hearty welcome'.[25]

In 1893 a rather delicate matter came into the public eye. One of Sam Redfern's sons, also on the music-hall stage and using the name Sam Redfern (it is not clear which, either Frederick or William), was cited as a co-respondent in a divorce case. It would appear that two years earlier Samuel Jones, whose stage name was Hugh Dempsey, unexpectedly came to London, after a tour in the north of England, to meet his wife, whose stage name was Lily Laurel. He found her in her nightdress in the bedroom with Sam Redfern the younger, who in court admitted to living with Lily Laurel. The judge awarded Jones his divorce and damages against Sam Redfern of £250. This caused Sam Redfern, the father, two problems. First, the confusion with the names had to be resolved in case it affected bookings and relationships with others in the profession, so a notice was published in the newspapers.[26] Second, the damages of £250 were substantial; most music-hall artistes earned £3 a week, when they had work, and out of that they had to pay expenses, for accommodation when touring and all their props.[27] A top name could command £200 a week on a good contract.[28] It is unlikely that the younger Sam Redfern, who was only 21 or 23, depending upon which one it was, at the time of the divorce case, would be able to pay that level of damages, so it is probable that the father had to help out in some way.

Poor investment of his savings also seemed to be a problem for Sam Redfern senior. In 1897 he forfeited shares in the Lancashire, Derbyshire and East Coast Railway Company for non-payment of calls for capital, which cost him £90.[29] He also seemed to enjoy buying paintings, which do not always appreciate in value and generate no income.[30] On 28 February 1908 at 11:30 a.m. in the Bankruptcy Buildings, Carey Street, London, there was a public examination of

Sam Redfern's finances. He declared that he had liabilities of £244 and assets were nil. He attributed his failure to losses in a poultry farm and a public house and an accident in a Coventry music hall which meant he could no longer work.[31]

Was the public house that contributed to Sam Redfern's financial failure the Mount Pleasant Hotel in Wombourne? Certainly it seems to fit many of the facts that we have.

In the 1901 census William, Sam's youngest son, is described as a public house manager. On the night the census was taken, the 31st of March 1901, it is clearly stated to be a hotel and not a public house, but there appear to be no guests. There were three staff living in the premises, a housekeeper, Eliza Banner, a groom and gardener, Thomas Amery, and a general servant, Mary Massey. With no income from guests this appears to be a lot of staff. Also, is there a hint that the hotel was aimed at a level of guest that might be difficult to find in Wombourne? A groom and gardener suggests horses needing to be cared for and gardens to be maintained. The competition in the village certainly seemed to operate on fewer staff: of the seven inns and public houses four had servants living in on the night of the census. The New Inn and the Swan Inn had only a single general servant. The Red Lion and the Vine had two servants, but for

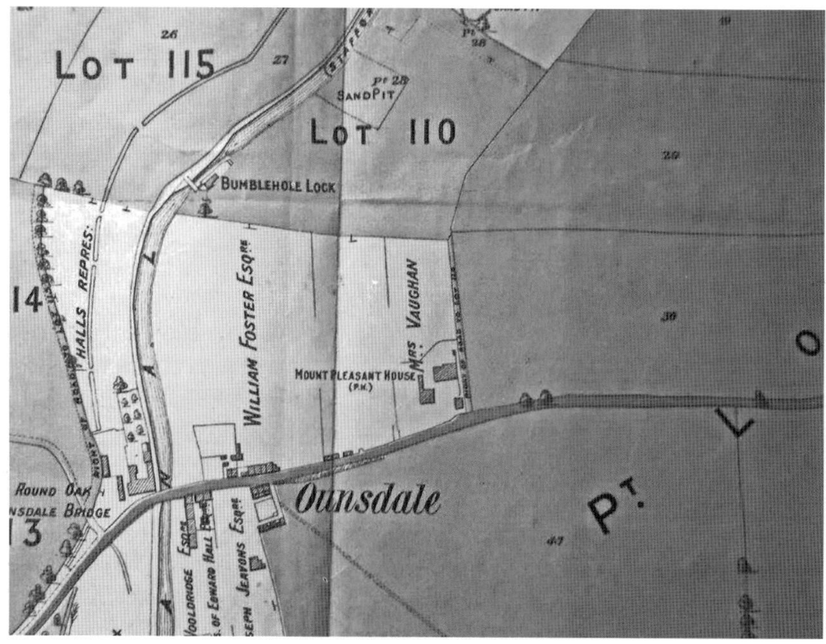

Map from an auctioneer's catalogue of 1910.

List of Licensees

*c.*1835–77	Richard Deans
1877–86	John Leedham
1886–89	Benjamin Ives
1894–97	Mary Vaughan
1897–1914	Samuel Redfern
1914–20	John Jones
1920–27	Samuel Gardiner
1927–31	Harry Huskin
1931–34	John T. Morrey
1934–38	Benjamin Clarke
1938–57	George T. Glover
1957–58	John M. Underwood
1958–60	John W. Sumpton
1960–74	Arthur L. Hubball
1974–75	Anne M. Deakin
1975–79	David A. Deakin
1979–91	William A. Morris
1991–200?	Anthony Clarke
2002–	James Gogarty

the Red Lion one was a brewer and ostler, so they brewed their own beer. The Vine had one guest on the night.

The Mount Pleasant Inn, as it is now known, has a list of all of its licensees and shows that Sam Redfern held the licence from 1897 to 1914. In the 1911 census the Mount Pleasant was still called a hotel, run by John Jones, his wife Margaret and his brother Walter. Again, no guests are recorded, but there are no servants either.

On 11 November 1910 Sam Redfern appeared before the High Court of Justice in Bankruptcy. His address is given as 131 St George's Road, Southwark, but had previously been 17 Grove Road, Brixton in Surrey. His bankruptcy in 1908 was being reviewed by the official receiver, who found that the 'bankrupt's assets are not of a value equal to 10s in the pound on the amount of his unsecured liabilities'. Therefore, the judge ordered that 'discharge [be] suspended for two years. Bankrupt to be discharged as from the 14th October, 1912'.[32]

In 1911 he was living at 36 Bridge Street, Walsall, with his wife Mary, his granddaughter Rosie and Lizzie Redfern Banner, his niece, working as a furniture dealer. Perhaps this story did end well for Sam Redfern. In 1914, as the First World War was starting and Belgian refugees were appearing in Britain, Belgian Relief Funds were established, Sam Redfern donating the not inconsiderable sum of £5.[33] He died in 1915. It would be nice to think that his patter and ability to engage an audience, built up on the stage, helped him to sell furniture in Walsall.

Bibliography

Norris, Peter, *A Cockney At Work – The Story Of Gus Elen And His Songs*, Grosvenor House Publishing, Guildford, 2014.

Notes

1 *The Era*, 4 August 1867, issue 1508.
2 *The Era*, 18 August 1867, issue 1508.
3 *The Era*, 1 November 1868, Issue 1571.
4 *The Era*, 30 January 1870, Issue 1636.
5 *The Era*, 25 September 1870, Issue 1668.
6 *The Era*, 29 January 1871, Issue 1688.
7 *The Era*, 29 September 1872, Issue 1775.
8 *The Era*, 9 April 1871, Issue 1698.
9 *The Era*, 5 May 1872, Issue 1754.
10 *The Era*, 2 June 1872, Issue 1758.
11 *The Era*, 11 May 1873, Issue 1807.
12 *The Era*, 27 December 1874, Issue 1892.
13 *The Era*, 3 January 1875, Issue 1893.
14 *The Era*, 27 June 1875, Issue 1918.
15 *The Era*, 12 December 1875, Issue 1942.
16 *The Era*, 28 January 1877, Issue 2001.
17 *The Penny Illustrated Paper*, 1 May 1886, Issue 1299.
18 *Manchester Times*, 17 November 1899, Issue 2206.
19 *Judy: The Conservative Comic*, 13 December 1893.
20 *The Sporting Times*, 13 January 1894, Issue 1582.
21 *The Era*, 18 August 1872, Issue 1769.
22 *The Birmingham Daily Post*, 17 December 1895, Issue 11700.
23 *The Standard*, 11 June 1889, Issue 20256.
24 *The Sporting Times*, 22 December 1894, Issue 1631, and 13 May 1899, Issue 1860.
25 *The Birmingham Daily Post*, 7 August 1900, Issue 13152.
26 *The Glasgow Herald*, 17 August 1893, Issue 196.
27 Peter Norris, *A Cockney At Work – The Story Of Gus Elen And His Songs*, Grosvenor House Publishing, Guildford, 2014, p.370.
28 Norris, p.259.
29 *London Gazette*, 1 October 1897, p.5390.
30 Norris, p.424.
31 *The Stage Year Book*, 1908, p.323.
32 *London Gazette*, 11 November 1910, p.8145.
33 *Manchester Guardian*, 2 September 1914, p.7.

Ernest Frederick Goodyear (1868–1947)

Philip Pennell

A trade directory of the early twentieth century contained the following fairly eye-catching entry. Under the heading 'Private Residents' appear:

> Goodyear Ernest Frederick: Park Mount (Inventor)
> Goodyear George William: Dunedin (Inventor)

Unfortunately, George William died shortly after the trade directory was published so his appearance in *Wombourne Worthies* is only a brief one.

Ernest Frederick was born in Dudley in 1868, the first child of William John and Mary Ellen Goodyear. His siblings John and Ellen were born in 1873 and 1877 respectively. The whole family lived together in the parish of St Thomas in Dudley until 1891 when Ernest Frederick married Minnie Millman who came from Kingswinford. It seems likely that after their marriage they moved into Park Mount which is situated on the A449. The house is now a care home. They appear to have lived there until the 1910s. In 1893 they had their eldest son Claude Eugene who, as we will see later, joined his father in the inventing profession.

In the 1911 census Ernest Frederick was shown as 'a file and tool manufacturer' and there is no doubt he worked at the Reliance Works, Dudley. This was the address of W. Goodyear and Sons, a family firm mentioned in Pigot's trade directory in 1828–29, which made bicycles or cycle wheels. The same census describes George William as 'engineer, file and tool manufacturer'. Pictures of products made by the company are featured in trade leaflets of the time.

However, by the early years of the twentieth century they had switched to motor car wheels The illustration is a 1920 advertisement showing wheels produced by the firm for the Morris car company. So it is hardly surprising that the first two patents with which the two engineers were associated were entitled 'improvements in

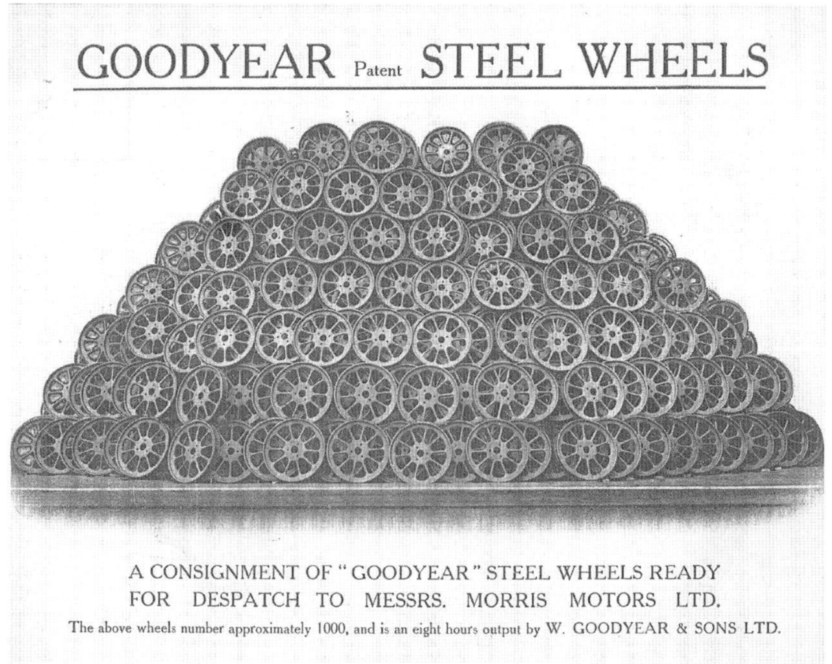

A CONSIGNMENT OF "GOODYEAR" STEEL WHEELS READY FOR DESPATCH TO MESSRS. MORRIS MOTORS LTD.
The above wheels number approximately 1000, and is an eight hours output by W. GOODYEAR & SONS LTD.

the manufacture of cycle forks' and 'certain improvements in or relating to wheels e.g. road wheels for autos etc.'. The latter was such a success that in 1907 HMSO produced a book about it. This had the somewhat long title of 'Original patent application number 10414 for improvements in and relating to wheel rims and in the means of securing tyres to the same (Wolverhampton)'. Ernest Frederick appears to have been the only author and Patent 10414 set him on his way to amassing forty patents to his name.

Four of them were invented for W. Goodyear and Sons, one in the pre-WWI period and three shortly after the end of the war. Whether this gap was caused by Ernest Frederick joining up or by the firm's efforts to help the war effort is not clear. All the patents are for auto wheels, but George William is noted as 'deceased' in the introduction to the first of them and Ernest Frederick's address is stated to be in Dudley. So it must be presumed he and his family left Wombourne around the time of the First World War. However, there is no doubt about the family's next move. This was in 1925, to Moxhull Park, Wishall, Warwickshire. (The site of this is now on the Belfry golf course.) In that same year the Dudley firm were taken over by an internationally known company.

Thus a person with the surname *Goodyear* joined *Dunlop* (the firm that had added W. Goodyear and Sons to their growing portfolio).

Ernest Frederick's workplace changed to Coventry where Dunlop's research department was situated and, as can be seen from the patents bearing his name, his work expanded to include aeroplane brakes, wheels and their controls.

It appears that he retired from Dunlop towards the end of the 1930s or early 1940s and moved house once more, this time to St Brelades, Wergs Road, Tettenhall (part of Wolverhampton) where he lived with his wife Minnie until both were into their 80s. But retirement did not mean that Ernest Frederick gave up inventing things. He joined up with his son Claude Eugene to design 'improvements in twin-rim disc wheels for vehicles' and, somewhat bizarrely, 'improvements in holders of sealing wax'. The last of these applications was submitted to the London patent office on 21 September 1945.

Ernest Frederick died aged 80 years and was buried in the graveyard of St Michael and All Angels, Tettenhall alongside his beloved wife Minnie.

Notes and References

1. Most of the information was taken from the American patents which can be found online.
2. Other sources include the English censuses, trade directories and Dudley Archives.
3. Fig. 1 O.S. Map 1900 published by Alan Godfrey Maps.
4. Figs. 2 and 3 Trade leaflets for W. Goodyear and Sons Ltd (from Dudley Archives).
5. Fig. 4 Advertisement for W. Goodyear and Sons Ltd (from Dudley Archives and Local History service).
6. Fig. 5 Gravestone of Ernest and Minnie Goodyear (from the website billion-graves. com).

John Apse – Headmaster of Wombourne School 1904–1946

Marian Innes

John Apse was born in Lydeard St Lawrence in Somerset in 1880 but it was teaching that brought him and his wife Florence to the Midlands. He taught for a short time at Claverley before being appointed headmaster of Wombourne School in 1904 where he remained in post until his retirement in 1946. He and Florence very quickly involved themselves in all aspects of village life until their deaths in 1961 and 1948 respectively.

John had many qualities and skills. As well as being headmaster he was a keen gardener and expert beekeeper, winning medals and

Boys and girls were taught beekeeping. John Apse was an accredited beekeeper.

trophies and eventually became a well-known and respected judge throughout the county. He was also interested in sport, participating in tennis and bowling as well as playing hockey and cricket for the village teams. Since 1910 the cricket, tennis and bowling clubs had been based on land at the centre of the village originally rented from the Shaw Hellier family. However, in 1945 the family bequeathed the site to the County Council with the stipulation that it remain as a permanent site for sport and recreation. Sports are still played there to the present day. Hockey was played on the Maypole Street side of the land until 1965 when they moved to Council land at Pendeford in Wolverhampton though still retaining 'Wombourne' as part of their name.

John was a committed Christian and attended St Benedict's Church where he served as one of the churchwardens, as well as councillor, treasurer and chorister for a good number of years. He had a deep melodious voice which carried easily and when it was his turn to read the lesson he did so with conviction, ably conveying the underlying message in such a way as to make it understandable and interesting for young and old alike. He had a charismatic quality that brought the parable alive and, as was the intention, made the congregation reflect and ponder their own behaviour.

Wombourne, as with most of the surrounding villages, had been putting on shows of various kinds for many years. These shows tended to take their origins from forerunners such as the Gooseberry Show which was held at the New Inn as early as 1813. John was instrumental in resurrecting the Wombourne Show in 1920 and it continued until its demise in 1968. During this time he was active in the planning and organisation of the show and held the office of chairman and other posts throughout this period. He was assisted by other keen gardeners and the ladies of the local branch of the Women's Institute. Almost everyone in the village attended and the show generated great excitement. It was noted that after 1947 when a horse show and gymkhana were added, as many as 10,000 people attended. In the 1930s local bus companies foresaw that there was profit to be made and offered incentives such as cheap tickets to encourage visitors to avail themselves of their service. Not that encouragement was needed as the attractions were many and varied. There were decorated cart competitions, sheepdog trials, motorcycle displays, horse jumping, acrobats and vendors on hand to thrill and astound. There was also whippet racing, and bookies, all ready to relieve hard-earned cash from the unwary, the naive and the foolish. For those attending this was a great day out, all for the price of one shilling for adults and six old pennies for children. There was always a dance in the village hall in the evening and those who came after seven o'clock for the dancing were allowed in at a reduced rate. As an enthusiastic amateur photographer John took his camera everywhere with him, recording events and thereby ensuring a tangible link between past and present for future generations to come.

Although John was of retirement age when WWII broke out he stayed on as headmaster having already seen the school through WWI. It must have been poignant for him to watch young men, many of whom he had taught as boys, going off to fight for their country. Never one to be idle, John was happy to do his bit for King and country during the WWII years. He served as chief Air-Raid Precautions officer and therefore was a pivotal figure at this tumultuous time, planning, dealing with emergencies and endeavouring to keep the villagers as safe as possible. During this time the Women's Institute hall was used for activities such as lectures detailing air raid precautions, emergency procedures as well as various money-raising events which helped support the war effort.

In 1925 the Great Western Railway had opened a line between Dunstall Park, Wolverhampton and Brettell Lane, Stourbridge, with a stopping-off point at Bratch station in Wombourne. After the allied forces landed in Normandy, the wounded were flown home and dispersed by rail to hospitals throughout the country. Thanks to its isolated location the Bratch was ideally situated to accommodate

John Apse in his 80s at his granddaughter's wedding.

hospital trains, where under cover of darkness the wounded could be transferred to ambulances in which volunteers transported them to hospitals in the region. Himley Hall was also used as a convalescent hospital. The last train departed on 13 June 1964 and the track is now a pleasant railway walk well used by residents of the village. A memorial was eventually unveiled in April 1920 to commemorate those thirty-eight individuals who had lost their lives during the WWI. John's feelings can only be imagined as he stood thirty years later when another eighteen names were inscribed into the same granite.

John was a handsome man. He had a sense of humour, a generous personality and those that knew him remembered the constant twinkle in his blue eyes. He and Florence had two children, a son John and a daughter Dorothy. As a couple they were well matched, both apparently being energetic and resourceful. Florence also taught at her husband's school, instilling into young girls the practical skills that they would need to run a household and make ends meet in those austere years. From all accounts she was an excellent cook, housewife, active sportswoman and member of the 1913 tennis team as well as a founder member of the Women's Institute where she held various posts over a twenty-eight-year period including that of secretary. Together John and Florence actively embraced life, mirroring qualities of fairness, honesty and justice.

When John was in his eighties the Parochial Church Council decided to honour him by naming a new gate from School Road into the churchyard after him and the *Apse Gate* still stands. This was done to commemorate his work and service to his school, his pupils and his lengthy contribution to village life. However, there was also a practical necessity attached to the deed. Previously, the top portion of the churchyard on Church Hill had been given to the village in 1901 at the time of the Lloyd Estate sale. The land came with the proviso that it could be used as a recreational ground for village activities until such time as the ground would be needed for additional space in the churchyard. Until the 1950s this portion of land had indeed been used for various functions such as parades, gatherings and had proved to be an excellent site for village bonfires and other occasions. It came to be affectionately known by the villagers as *The Rec.* Following the population explosion after the Second World War additional grave space was needed so The Rec was consecrated as an extension to the existing graveyard and at the same time a hedge was planted on School Road. However, the steepness of the hill was a problem as it made carrying a coffin up the hill difficult, especially in winter weather. To overcome this, a gateway was created through the hedge enabling the undertakers to drive the hearse through into the new churchyard, thereby making life easier for all concerned.

The gate is still in use today though the original wooden one has now been replaced by one made of wrought iron.

The vicar that presided over the dedication ceremony was the Reverend Walter Bethway, and it must have been a source of amusement for those attending to witness John being present at his own 'memorial' service. After his death John Apse was further honoured when the Parish Council named *Apse Close* in his memory. Apse Close is a cul-de-sac situated at Mount Pleasant Avenue, near the pub of the same name on Ounsdale Road.

Schooldays

While John's many qualities were apparent in his activities in village and family life it was in his role of headmaster that he excelled. John commenced his duties on July 1, 1904, immediately after the school had been closed for a total of eight weeks due to a measles epidemic. Such epidemics were not unusual in the early twentieth century; teachers had to be vigilant and look for signs of diseases such as diphtheria, scarlet fever, whooping cough and measles and take appropriate preventative action to contain outbreaks. On his very first day at the school John made his mark by purchasing new desks, books and maps. He also changed the timetable by closing the school at four p.m. to allow those children who had to travel long distances, usually on foot, to get home safely. This was very necessary as evidenced by school logs written in John's neat hand over 100 years ago, which reported on harsh conditions:

> *March 4th, 1909 – School not opened, weather unfit, severe snow storm*
>
> *January 18th, 1912 – Deep snow this morning and still snowing. Only 80 children present of which 8 were immediately sent home and the remainder arranged round the fires where clothes and boots had to be dried. The weather being worse in the afternoon the children were dismissed and the school closed for the remainder of the week.*

The two playgrounds behind the school were separated by a brick wall. One was for girls and one for boys, each with their own toilet accommodation. The recreational ground, 'The Rec', opposite the school provided additional playground space and a sports field. This was especially beneficial to the children in the summer months because it provided an ideal picnic area where children could sit, have their lunch and play games. The row of elm trees which stood along School Road at that time had a wall between them and the road. Into this wall white iron posts had been embedded with chains linking each post and this provided an ideal swing area and was well used. Crossing the road was not hazardous as there was very little

School staff prior to First World War.
John Apse front row 2nd left.
Mrs Apse back row 2nd left.

traffic then. Crossing beacons were not introduced until 1934 by the then Minister of Transport, Leslie Hore-Belisha, and they became known as Belisha beacons.

John set about diversifying the curriculum and while a focus on the three Rs was important he also introduced many new subjects. The county education advisors were contacted about acquiring a school garden and one was established in the field beyond the school premises. Work began on cultivation in the autumn and the education process was in operation by the spring of the following year. Boys were taught to graft fruit trees and grow vegetables in rotation so that there was an abundant supply throughout the year. Products were then used in Florence's cookery classes. On April 19, 1910 a deputation from West Africa visited the school and were most impressed by the school garden and the work done by the boys. It can only be hoped that the West African children benefited from the occasion. Under John's keen eye the school garden was a great success – so much so that other schools in the area followed suit and started to cultivate their own plots of land. On March 11 in 1911 the school received a fowl house, plus five white Orpington pullets and a cockerel, thus extending the range of husbandry taught.

Other crafts included dressmaking, rug-making, painting and drawing. Leisure pursuits such as country dancing were held during the summer months on the lawn in the school garden. In addition there was cricket, netball and rounders with school teams competing in local leagues. A football team was also established in 1905. The football was bought using money from the boys' subscriptions and some additional finance from John and the local vicar. His enthusiasm was infectious and transferred itself to the young people who, in turn, rewarded him by excelling and winning trophies in a number of competitions. The country dance team won acclamation and certificates at the Country Music Association and the Wolverhampton Dance Society. A school choir was formed and this became a permanent fixture with youngsters participating at many celebratory and church events.

Every summer John would bring an observation hive into the school. This consisted of an upright wooden frame with glass sides into which he would put bees and some honeycomb. Children could then watch the bees bringing in the honey, feeding the baby grubs, filling the neat little wax cells and waiting on the queen. He also brought in full honeycombs and hung them in an extractor shaped like a large metal urn with a handle at the top. When the lid was in place and the handle turned the honeycombs spun round inside, thus allowing honey to be extracted. This was an extra-curricular activity that paid dividends depending upon how much honey could be accumulated on little fingers and how delicious it tended to taste when licked.

There were summer walks round the village, accompanied by a teacher. On these pupils learned to recognise the different species of trees, the names of all the wild flowers and how to respect the

Mrs Apse with her cookery class in 1917.

abundance of wildlife that lived along the Wom Brook from which the village derived its name. John made sure every youngster was enrolled for the wild grass and flower classes and encouraged them to take part in the village show. The brook provided a safe haven for water voles and moorhens that nested in its nooks and crannies as well as the myriad of insects including the blue-tailed damselfly, the bumblebee and the orange-tipped butterflies that darted in and out of the vegetation along its banks. The canal was another source of delight with its brightly painted houseboats and friendly occupants chugging along at a leisurely pace, content to enjoy the peace and tranquillity of the English countryside.

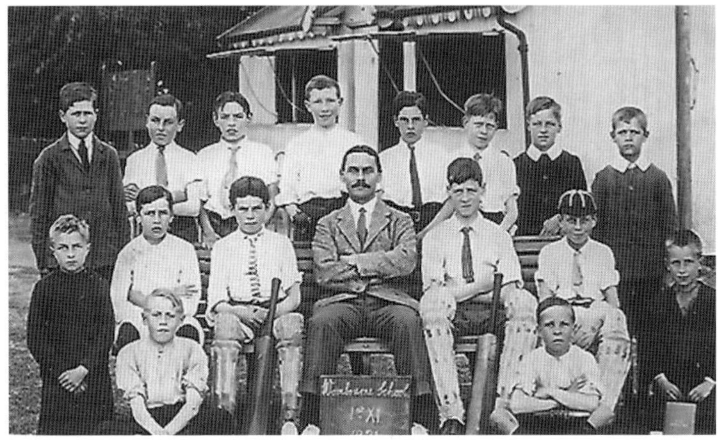

The 1st XI cricket team in 1921 with John Apse

The 1st XI football team 1920/21. John Apse 2nd from left back row.

For every child there was one special occasion which was the highlight of the school year. This was the annual school outing, though in essence it was a village outing. Not just the children, but parents, uncles, aunts, grandparents and any other individual, no matter how tenuous the connection to the genealogical tree, contrived to be part of this special day. This was John's *pièce de résistance*, his crowning glory and his jewel in the crown. He was very much aware that those young people attending his school came from mixed backgrounds and for many families life was harsh and money tight. Some children and adults had never been outside the village boundaries, so what better way was there to broaden their horizons than a trip to the seaside? From the start of the September term children took a few pence, or whatever they could afford, to school each week. The sum was duly recorded in a register so that by the following summer enough would have been saved to cover costs. If a family by some misfortune fell short of missing the target it was John who provided that little bit extra to ensure that no child was left out.

Once a destination had been agreed, John, ever the teacher, provided each child with a plain postcard detailing the towns en route and opposite each he would put the products or buildings associated with it. On the flip side was the day's itinerary, the time of departure, arrival, stopping-off points and when they could expect to be back. Nothing was left to chance, and a year's organising meant every eventuality was planned for. Each year John booked a train consisting of fourteen Great Western carriages all linked by one corridor. Departure from the village station at the Bratch had to be early so that the coast could be reached as soon as possible. Foxes on their way home from a night's hunting must have stopped and marvelled at the noise emanating from a crowd of excited, happy humans gathered in the grey light of dawn waiting for that first glimpse of smoke which would herald the start of a much-anticipated adventure. Even on this day John would don the mantle of responsibility by meticulously ticking off each name before boarding commenced. When this task was completed he would make sure each door was firmly secured before giving the nod to the guard who then waved his flag, blew his whistle and sent them off. What magical destinations these were: Brighton, Weymouth, Torquay, the resorts of the Welsh coast – names on a map – and all so far away.

The joy of that journey was enhanced by the fact that everybody knew everybody else. There was time for the adults to catch up with old friends, gossip to be exchanged. The children ran up and down the corridor, played hide and seek and made new best friends until there was the first tantalising glimpse of water: the sea. Then there was the hurried scramble to gather belongings, the frustrating wait until the train stopped, the doors were opened and then the happy frenzy as a hoard of children competed to be first out the door and onto the beach. So much to do, no time to waste. The pleasure of children living in the moment and savouring the taste, tang and touch of salt water on feet and hands was a delight to behold. They paddled, bathed, marvelled at the tiny fishes that darted through the waves, avoided the crabs with their fearsome pincers, prodded the jellyfish and explored rock pools left by the departing tide where they uncovered the strange and fascinating creatures that rested in the shadows. The consistency of the soft wet sand was made for building castles or just for digging. Shapely shells scattered randomly on the beach were meant to be brought home as souvenirs.

Then there was the promenade with its crazy golf, stalls and shops offering brightly coloured candyfloss, ice cream, toffee apples, sweets in brightly coloured jars, balloons blowing in the breeze, the array of trinkets as well as the slot machines offering inducements, the peep shows promising an insight into 'what the butler saw', concoctions of every description to bewitch and bewilder. Young legs made short shrift of the long walk to the end of the pier for the obligatory boat trip. For those who could not afford such a luxury they made do with just watching fishermen as they landed their catch while talking to each other in a strange accent. John was everywhere with his camera, snapping those happy moments for posterity. Finally, everyone poured onto the train for the return journey home tired, subdued but happy, and content in knowing that next year it would happen all over again.

John was a man of his time and he lived in his time. He was scrupulously fair in his dealings with those in his care. Rules had to be obeyed and he made sure that the underlying purpose of that rule was understood and accepted. He made pupils appreciate that for every action there is a consequence. Human nature being what it is, there were always those who tested limits – that is how experience is gained. Retribution, when meted out, was done not with the intent of suppressing a young adventurous spirit but in the hope that channelling it in the direction most suited to the characteristics and flair of the recipient would make it work for them and not against them. John was a born leader and a natural teacher. The children respected him, listened to the wisdom of his words and tried to emulate his actions. Perhaps that is why, when in later years with schooldays long gone, and they themselves had children of their own, they still affectionately referred to him as 'the gaffer'. Under his tutelage, learning was not confined to the classroom but also encompassed those skills needed to live through war and its aftermath, depression, the General Strike of 1926 and the turbulent years leading up to the next war. John was aware that life is all memory apart from that one present moment that flits by so fast you hardly catch it going. His greatest legacy was that he left happy memories, magic moments that made up happy days. For him every day was special, every place was a special place, and he was special to Wombourne.

He lived in an era accepting its limitations and embracing its changes. He had owned one of the first motor vehicles in Wombourne and in his seventies could be seen on many an occasion driving his car, E6867, through Wombourne streets and beyond. In his eighties, dapper, handsome and still with that mischievous twinkle in his eye, he can be seen about to attend the wedding of his granddaughter shortly before he died aged 81 in 1961. Florence died, aged 69, in 1948. They are both buried in the same grave in St Benedict's churchyard. John Apse was a remarkable man and one worthy of remembrance by those privileged to have known him.

John in one of Wombourne's first cars.

Index

Page numbers in *italics* refer to illustrations

Index

Index